THE ARCHITECTURE OF
LITERACY
THE CARNEGIE LIBRARIES
OF NEW YORK CITY

by Mary B. Dierickx

Honorable Rudolph W. Giuliani, Mayor of the City of New York
The Cooper Union for the Advancement of Science and Art
New York City Department of General Services
New York City Department of Design and Construction
Brooklyn Public Library
The New York Public Library
The Queens Borough Public Library

Contemporary Photographs by Lisa Clifford

This project was funded by the Arthur Ross Foundation and Furthermore, the J.M. Kaplan Fund publication program.

September 1, 1996

ISBN 1-56256-717-9

Printed in the United States of America

10 9 8 7 6 5 4 3 2 1

Cover image: *Hudson Park Branch Library, Leroy Street Entrance, c. 1910, Lewis
Hine Photographer (Archives of The New York Public Library Astor, Lenox and
Tilden Foundations)*

TABLE OF CONTENTS

The Queens Borough Public Library

203   Appendix

September 1, 1996

Dear Friends:

I am pleased to recognize the publication of *The Architecture of Literacy: The Carnegie Libraries of New York City*. Andrew Carnegie's belief in the importance of libraries and his generous philanthropic contributions enabled the construction of public libraries throughout the world. We are fortunate to have the largest collection of Andrew Carnegie libraries here in New York City. Our libraries are community resources that provide all New Yorkers with the opportunity to educate themselves and improve their quality of life. On behalf of the residents of New York City, I commend those associated with the production of this work for continuing the historic preservation of New York City architecture. *The Architecture of Literacy* will ensure that the Carnegie libraries will be preserved for generations to come.

Sincerely,

Rudolph W. Giuliani
Mayor

Yorkville Branch Library, 222 East 79th Street, 1992
Sketch by Saija Singer, Cooper Union '96

September 1, 1996

Dear New Yorkers:

As an institution that has shaped the discourse, study and practice of art and architecture for more than a century, The Cooper Union for the Advancement of Science and Art is pleased to be the sponsoring organization for *The Architecture of Literacy*. This comprehensive study celebrates one of the City's great legacies: the magnificent libraries of Andrew Carnegie.

It should come as no surprise that an institution founded by Peter Cooper should be partner to this project. As a passionate New Yorker who made generous contributions to civic life, Cooper inspired many other citizens of his time to do the same. He established a "Union" which, to this day, offers a full scholarship education to meritorious students, regardless of their economic or cultural circumstances.

Andrew Carnegie shared Peter Cooper's zealous public spirit which fostered inclusiveness in learning. Carnegie's own lasting contribution was nothing short of extraordinary: the development of hundreds of free libraries throughout New York (and, indeed, the world). These citadels have endured as community outposts for knowledge and scholarship, open to all.

This publication rightly commemorates the role that these two visionaries, Carnegie and Cooper, played in shaping civic institutions dedicated to the democratic principles of community service and free access to education and culture.

Cooper Union has also been pleased to share two of its talented students of architecture with the project. Saija Singer and Yvette Nesbeth have provided valuable assistance to project director Mary Dierickx, while enriching their own learning experiences through researching and documenting the buildings.

The project owes its inspiration to Kenneth B. Miller, a descendent of Andrew Carnegie and a citizen of New York City. In its realization, *The Architecture of Literacy* represents a rewarding collaboration among public and private entities, government and borough offices, and individuals. The participants have contributed to encourage New Yorkers' understanding of the significance and value of Carnegie's contribution to the well being of their City.

Our hope is that this publication will serve as a guide for those concerned with honoring and preserving the built environment, as well as a resource for those dedicated to the public good.

Sincerely,

John Jay Iselin
President
THE COOPER UNION

Dear Library Friends:

There's still room for understanding libraries. Recently the economic development officer of Southwestern Pennsylvania escorted a visiting CEO around Pittsburgh and its environs, hoping to locate a suitable plant site. After several hours of touring, the CEO remarked "Andrew Carnegie was a very rich man, wasn't he?" "Yes," was the reply. Then after a long pause, the CEO elaborated. "What I cannot understand," he said "is how he made so much money running a chain of libraries."

Social concerns inspired Carnegie's library building program. He believed this country and the world would be a better place with free, universal access to information, universal literacy for our diverse population, and encouragement for those who would help themselves. The libraries he provided were built with this in mind, addressing spiritual and physical concerns, sited according to marketing sense, and constructed following community need-based design. These social concerns and their attendant architectural principles are a lesson not only for modern library planning worldwide, but equally for new structures of electronic connectedness—the architecture of learning—for the next century.

Institutions evolve, and the Carnegie libraries of New York like libraries nationwide, faced with constrained budgets, new notions of community, and rapidly changing information technology, have had to recast missions, adjust programs, and especially in the communities with foresight, where the buildings are older, unravel the competing lines of traditional and modern services. This is a familiar process. Every decade this century you can find headlines telling the same story—the need for money and upgraded buildings. But this time the libraries might just be undergoing systemic change. This time the technological moves—how we find and use information and entertain ourselves cannot be countered with extended hours of library service alone or even by adding traditional programs. The information explosion is mature (it started at least as early as 1850), but now we are undergoing a paradigm shift in how we deal with both the information explosion and the social fractures of late 20th century life. Business and recreational life in the 21st century increasingly will be spent online, using the speed and process intelligence of interactivity, gathering information, but also seeking ideas, answers, popular opinion, and relationships from cyberspace.

People who dwell in cyberspace are changed by the experience. The Internet's nodal network, made up of an evolving class of electronic media, is helping people communicate one-to-one, one-to-many, and many-to-many, facilitating not just the free exchange of information, but also encouraging online and offline discourse, argument, serving as a gateway to other worlds, across borders, an environment of self-help, color-blind, a place to acquire citizenship skills, and at its best promoting informed opinion fundamental to democracy.

The first public libraries, many of the Carnegies sited purposefully at the center of a community, on a highly visible corner, with mind-clearing approaches and vaulted interiors supportive of reading, focused thought, and ennobled discussion, also served this town-hall function. Carnegie libraries in 67 communities around New York were nodes of a community architecture, each adapted to the local neighborhood and realized with aid from local librarians and community leaders, but sharing common strengths of design and function. Each building is explicitly an advocate for space which serves common and individual purpose without bias.

This is a particularly worthwhile time to be studying an architectural heritage which has worked well for nearly 100 years, for in the process of unfolding the Internet, largely an organic human enterprise, there's at least one cyber banana peel. Like Superman's Crystal Palace, the Net's architecture is magically taking shape too fast and according to rules too complex to appreciate how its forms will affect our lives (which has not stopped people from explaining it). Yet the underlying architecture of the Net (as apart from what you see on the Net) is increasingly designed by a few very few information managers and politicians. A few people are circumscribing the architecture of the new meeting place, its capability and capacity, and its economics, and this action ultimately will bind us all (in cyberspace, every individual is potentially a publisher as well as a learner). In the tradition of great common space champions through history, those who raise their voices for openness in the Internet are also architects. Those who champion free access to the Net are framers of the continuing democratic revolution.

Talking about the Carnegie libraries of New York as a collection of buildings risks placing them in our thinking as museum pieces. This they are decidedly not. Their architectural interest—even excellence—belies their forceful role in each community, as vessels of learning, birthing young thinkers. That they are also tracks of our culture, living ciphers, illuminating a process of extraordinary achievement fueled by absolute faith in the power of the individual, given opportunity, to change history and improve the lot of humankind, argues for their preservation, study, sensitive reworking, and collective respect. In the 2509 Carnegie libraries worldwide, some two hundred million users have tallied the success of this architecture. A careful study like Missy Dierickx's reveals what is right about these buildings. As we update the buildings or design our new architecture of learning, it's helpful to have what works in mind.

At a time when it's easy to justify frustration and impatience with the processes of city governance, the process by which this small but important piece of research was accomplished with modest resources is encouraging. It echoes the public-private partnership that Carnegie whipped into action with his original gift. A university, three library systems, a government agency, two private foundations, a scholar, and concerned citizens cooperated to see it through. Newton Minow, chair of the board of trustees of Carnegie Corporation and long in public service, tells a story about the cultured old gentleman walking with a gardener. He stops, points decisively to a spot in the earth, and says urgently "Plant this special tree here tomorrow morning." The gardener protests. "But this tree will not blossom for 100 years." Replies the gentleman, "In that case, you better plant it this afternoon." The vision of individuals designing a better world is sound. This research moves us forward, today.

Kenneth B. Miller

Kenneth B. Miller
Mr. Miller is President of Miller Associates, Inc., a software publisher and Chairman, Cooper-Hewitt, National Design Museum, Smithsonian Institution. Andrew Carnegie was his great-grandfather.

Tottenville Branch Library, 7430 Amboy Road, 1995,
Lisa Clifford, DGS Photographer

September 1, 1996

Dear New Yorkers:

The City of New York has been richly endowed with some of the finest Carnegie libraries in the nation, designed by some of America's most gifted architects. As cities and towns across the United States approach the centennials of the Carnegie libraries, our City, under the auspices of Mayor Rudolph W. Giuliani, has prepared *The Architecture of Literacy: The Carnegie Libraries of New York City*. We have gathered together a concerned constituency of City officials, community citizens and advocates, to initiate a program of City–wide activities to enrich this collection of buildings and to seek their preservation.

New York City has been greatly enriched by the intellectual and architectural legacy of Andrew Carnegie, who had the vision to establish sixty–seven libraries in our City, as well as thousands more throughout the nation and the world. It is our hope that the presentation of *The Architecture of Literacy* will be a re–dedication to the Carnegie libraries as vessels of learning, culture and literacy.

Sincerely,

William J. Diamond, Commissioner
NYC Department of General Services

Luis M. Tormenta, P.E., Commissioner
NYC Department of Design
and Construction

Edwin S. Holmgren, Director
The Branch Libraries
The New York Public Library

Martín Gómez, Executive Director
Brooklyn Public Library

Gary E. Strong, Director
The Queens Borough Public Library

ACKNOWLEDGEMENTS

A PARTNERSHIP FOR THE CARNEGIE LIBRARIES

The Cooper Union for the Advancement of Science and Art and the NYC Department of General Services appreciate the generous grants that made it possible to create *The Architecture of Literacy: The Carnegie Libraries of New York City,* with special thanks to Joan K. Davidson and Furthermore, the J.M. Kaplan Fund publication program, for supporting quality printing and distribution and to the Arthur Ross Foundation for making possible the extensive research and documentation for this unique publication. Special thanks are given to Kenneth B. Miller, great-grandson of Andrew Carnegie and Chairman of Cooper–Hewitt National Design Museum, Smithsonian Institution, who has been supportive of this work from inception to completion.

We wish to thank Mayor Rudolph W. Giuliani, Deputy Mayor Peter J. Powers and Deputy Mayor Fran Reiter who continue to provide priority and commitment to the Carnegie libraries as well as to the entire library system. In addition, credit must be shared with Borough Presidents Fernando Ferrer, Howard Golden, Ruth Messinger, Guy V. Molinari and Claire Shulman who have supported the preservation, utilization and development of the public libraries of New York City.

John Jay Iselin, President, The Cooper Union for the Advancement of Science and Art and William J. Diamond, Commissioner, NYC Department of General Services, deserve recognition for bringing about this public/private partnership to study and document the Carnegie libraries. Luis M. Tormenta P.E., appointed the Acting Commissioner of the NYC Department of Design and Construction in December 1995, is pleased to carry this effort forward with the enthusiastic collaboration of the three NYC library systems. Paul LeClerc, President of The New York Public Library; Bonnie Bellamy, President of the Brooklyn Public Library and Joel A. Miele, Sr., President of The Queens Borough Public Library are to be commended for their effort in bringing the Carnegie libraries story to everyone's attention.

Adrienne Bresnan, FAIA, Assistant Commissioner and Hannah McAninch, Deputy Director, NYC Department of General Services Historic Preservation Office were primarily responsible for spearheading this partnering effort and related activities to celebrate the Carnegie libraries in 1996. Lisa Clifford, DGS photographer performed the important function of documenting the Carnegie Libraries in the 1990s and John Yue, Director of Graphic Services for CityGraphics, developed the valuable graphic design concept with the Preservation Office.

Peoples Publishing, one of the largest multicultural publishers of educational textbooks, deserves a great deal of thanks for all their pro bono contribution of graphic design services, especially Diane Miller and Doreen Smith, who carried this work to the point where it could be of greatest value to the public. Thanks also to Henry Ballone, Brook Litho, for providing equipment and technical advice.

Many people have contributed significantly to this partnership effort:

The Cooper Union for the Advancement of Science and Art
John Jay Iselin, President
Camilla Brooks, Senior Development Officer, Art and Architecture
Richard Henderson AIA, Associate Dean, The Irwin S. Chanin School of Architecture
Karen Jewett, Program Manager, Extended Studies
Sean Sculley, Associate Professor Adjunct, The Irwin S. Chanin School of Architecture
Melissa Benca, Internship Coordinator
Yvette Nesbeth and Saija Singer, Student Interns

The NYC Department of General Services
William J. Diamond, Commissioner
Luis M. Tormenta, PE, 1st Asst. Commissioner
Michael J. Burton, PE, Deputy Commissioner
Anne Papageorge, RLA, Asst. Commissioner
Adrienne Bresnan, FAIA, Asst. Commissioner
Hillary Brown, RA, Asst. Commissioner
Joanna Pestka, AIA, Deputy Asst. Commissioner
Elisabeth Martin, AIA, Program Director, Libraries
Hannah McAninch, Asst. Director, Preservation
Christopher J. Lane, Deputy Commissioner
Carol J. Green, Purch. Dir., Municipal Supplies & Al Gil
Paula Young, Director, Communications
Lisa Clifford, Photographer
John Yue, Director, CityGraphics
Barry Steinman & Conrad Nunnally, CityGraphics
Frank Brady, Director, Records Management

The New York Public Library
Edwin S. Holmgren, Senior Vice President and Director, The Branch Libraries
Sandra L. Polsak, Director, Plant Management and Construction
Gennie Peréz, Branch Libraries Operations Manager
Robert E. Sink, Archivist/Records Manager

Brooklyn Public Library
Martín Goméz, Executive Director
Frank DeRosa, Director, Facilities Management and Risk Control
Helmut Hutter, Assistant Architect, Facilities Management and Risk Control
Judy Walsh, Local History Librarian

The Queens Borough Public Library
Gary E. Strong, Director
Kenneth G. Sivulich, Deputy Director
Robert J. Waters, Director of Engineering and Facilities Planning
Charles Young, Manager, Long Island Division

Landmarks Preservation Commission
Jennifer J. Raab, Commissioner

The Art Commission of the City of New York
Nicholas Quennell, President
Vivian M. Warfield, Executive Director

There are also individuals who deserve special acknowledgement for their role in the initiation of this work. They are former Mayor David N. Dinkins, Barbara J. Fife, Anthony R. Smith, Lynn Argenziano, Nanette Smith, Laurie Beckelman, Constance Cook, Larry Brandwein, Roy Miller, George S. Bobinski, Lenore Lucey FAIA, Sarelle Weisberg FAIA, Beverly Wilson, Marilyn Rispoli and Joseph Bresnan, FAIA.

We especially wish to thank Mary B. Dierickx, President of Mary B. Dierickx, Architectural Preservation Consultants, who gave so much more than was asked of her. Her passion for and devotion to historic preservation of NYC's architectural patrimony has resulted in a publication that not only celebrates the Carnegie libraries, but enhances our understanding and appreciation of this city's three great library systems. Jeffrey Baumoel provided additional research. Joseph Pell Lombardi, a NYC architect and Joseph Wall, former Professor Emeritus of History at Grinnell College and biographer of Andrew Carnegie, advised on the project.

Chatham Square Branch Library, 33 East Broadway, c. 1910
Children's Program, Lewis Hine Photographer
(Archives of The New York Public Library Astor, Lenox and Tilden Foundations)

INTRODUCTION

New York City has the largest collection of Carnegie libraries of any city in the country. There were 67 Carnegie branch libraries constructed between 1901 and 1929; 57 are still standing and 54 of those are still operating as libraries today. The buildings were designed by the finest architects in the U.S. and in New York: McKim, Mead & White; Carrere & Hastings; James Brown Lord; Babb, Cook & Willard, and Lord & Hewlett. The worldwide Carnegie library collection, a coherent architectural assemblage of over 2500 late 19th and early 20th century structures built through the philanthropy of Andrew Carnegie, has been widely acknowledged as a major force for social welfare and literacy.

While the entire Carnegie building program has been extensively studied, there has been no concentration on the exceptional New York City collection and no undertaking to interpret them to the public until today. The libraries continue to be enormously important to the City as a whole and to the communities they serve. This study will present the significance of these libraries to the public through description, illustrations and historical information in an accessible publication. The City will spend over $20 million in the next five to eight years for restoration, rehabilitation and programming improvements for the Carnegie branches. This study defines the essential characteristics of the collection for use in the planning and design of the current renovations, so that these irreplaceable libraries can be preserved for future generations.

Andrew Carnegie donated $5.2 million to New York City in 1901 to build a comprehensive branch library system in all five boroughs. This was a record library donation not just for Andrew Carnegie but for any single donor. The branch buildings were designed as a collection, with similar plans, materials, and style. The design of the structures represented a unique collaboration between architects and librarians on the plans, overall design and siting of the buildings. While there is significant variation in the details, the libraries read as a collection and can be easily identified as Carnegie branches, following the initial intention of the program.

This study is an historical, cultural and architectural overview of the New York City Carnegie libraries. The assessment takes into account the history and philosophy of Andrew Carnegie in the library movement, the commissioning of the buildings, and the role of the libraries in the community. The major features of the Carnegie libraries - what unifies them and what makes them special - are explored. In this study, the year of the official opening is used as the date of the library. The buildings were finished and opened, in most cases, within two or three years of their initial planning and design. The branch opening, which was accomplished with great ceremony and followed immediately by intensive use of the building, is the most significant individual date for these libraries.

Combining documentary and field research, the essay owes a debt to the several excellent publications on Carnegie libraries, listed in the bibliography. Additional information is also derived from primary and secondary sources within NYC institutions, in particular the collections of The New York Public Library, the Brooklyn Public Library, The Queens Borough Public Library and the New York City Department of General Services. Each of the extant Carnegie libraries in New York City was surveyed in the field and photographed.

This publication begins with letters from the participating institutions and individuals, and acknowledgements of the many people, agencies and institutions who have labored to make this study possible. An introduction explains the project. There is an essay summarizing the establishment and building of the Carnegie branches, as well as the philosophy behind their donation by Andrew Carnegie. The essay is illustrated with historic photos selected from the immensely significant collections of the three library corporations as well as historic and contemporary drawings, including interpretive sketches by Cooper Union student Saija Singer. Photographs in the New York Public Library collection by the famous photographer Lewis Hine are published here for the first time. A comprehensive list of the Carnegie libraries follows the essay.

Stone Avenue Branch Library, n.d., c. 1905
581 Stone Avenue
This library was originally the Brownsville Children's Branch, opened in 1914 to relieve overcrowding at the
Brownsville Branch. (Brooklyn Public Library, Brooklyn Collection)

The final section of the publication is devoted to the inventory of Carnegie libraries. This survey consists of a data sheet on each of the buildings, including libraries no longer standing, accompanied by contemporary and historic photographs. The information on the data sheets, derived primarily from the library archives, is meant to give the reader a snapshot of each building which, taken as a portfolio, provides an overview of the collection. The inventory sheets include the address, architect, date, an explanation of how the building fits into the neighborhood, a brief architectural description of the major original features and alterations, a few historical notes, the current use, and any future plans for restoration or rehabilitation.

The inventory section is divided by library system and by borough. A borough map provides the locations of the Carnegie branches in relation to the rest of the libraries in New York City. An appendix contains a selected bibliography, lists of the original architects and contractors, and the text of the original 1901 agreement between New York City and The New York Public Library.

The work of this document was funded through the generosity of the Arthur Ross Foundation and the Furthermore program of the J.M. Kaplan Fund and resulted in a very special partnership of The Cooper Union of the Advancement of Science & Art with four public sector agencies: the New York City Department of General Services, The New York Public Library, the Brooklyn Public Library and The Queens Borough Public Library. Kenneth Miller, great-grandson of Andrew Carnegie, had an invaluable role in bringing the work to fruition.

This publication is the second effort by the Historic Preservation Office of the New York City Department of General Services to document and analyze collections of New York City's public buildings. This ongoing effort of the Historic Preservation Office, with Adrienne Bresnan's vision and Hannah McAninch's guidance, began with *The Architecture of Public Justice*, a survey of the historic courthouses of the City of New York.

As cities and towns across the United States celebrate the approaching Centennials of their Carnegie libraries, *The Architecture of Literacy* can provide New York City, its well-read citizens and its public officials with a timely document to commemorate the Carnegies as well as to help preserve them as vessels of learning today and for the next one hundred years.

Mary B. Dierickx, 1996

Seward Park Branch Library, 192 East Broadway, 1992
Sketch by Saija Singer, Cooper Union '96

OVERVIEW

Andrew Carnegie

Andrew Carnegie was responsible for donating funds for over 1600 libraries in the United States and for initiating a comprehensive branch library system in New York City, donating $5.2 million dollars for 67 branches built between 1901 and 1929. Born in Scotland in 1835, he emigrated to the United States with his family when he was thirteen. His first job was in a textile mill in the famous - literally - rags to riches tale. In 1901, just over 50 years later, already one of the richest men in the world, he sold his steel company to J.P. Morgan for almost half a billion dollars.

Andrew Carnegie credited his rise from laborer in a textile mill to steel magnate to hard work and unrelenting self-improvement, recounting stories of productive days in his youth spent in the private library of Colonel Anderson in Allegheny City, Pennsylvania. He developed a philosophy of wealth and philanthropy, which was written in a private memo when he was just 33 and published as early as 1889. In it he noted that "Man must have an idol - the amassing of wealth is one of the worst species of idolatry - no idol more debasing than the worship of money."[1] In his 1889 Gospel of Wealth he stated that the wealthy should live simply, provide moderately for their families and then, while still living, act as trustees of their wealth, giving away their funds for the common good of humanity. He was to give away about 90% of his wealth and to do it with great efficiency. When he gave a library to a town, he insisted that the municipality provide the site and the maintenance, making the town's investment far greater than his own. He stated that this "was not philanthropy but a clever stroke of business."[2]

Carnegie believed in helping those who would help themselves by providing the means for them to improve themselves and their condition. He considered seven areas worthy of philanthropic attention: universities, libraries, medical centers, parks, meeting and concert halls, public baths, and churches.[3] Of the over $330 million Carnegie gave away, $40 million went to libraries.

Carnegie began his library donations in 1881 in Scotland with a grant to build a library in his home town of Dunfermline. His early giving was close to home in Pennsylvania and Scotland. He donated and endowed libraries in Allegheny, Johnstown and Homestead in Pennsylvania, and the Carnegie Institute and Library in Pittsburgh. His giving style in this early period was typical of late 19th century philanthropists who gave locally and in the area where they had close ties.

Libraries were a popular avenue for bequests and about $36 million was contributed in the last 20 years of the 19th century.[4] Philanthropists such as Walter Newberry in Chicago, George Peabody in Boston, and Charles Bower Winn in Massachusetts were noted for their library donations. The Astor and Lenox Libraries, which with the Tilden Trust formed the original New York Public Library, were created by the Astor, Lenox and Tilden families in the 19th century. Enoch Pratt gave $1 million to Baltimore with the provision that the City spend 5% of the grant on support of the libraries. Andrew Carnegie would later expand this concept for his giving.

With his broad philosophy and using the efficiency and practicality he showed in business, where he invented cost accounting, Andrew Carnegie moved well beyond this traditional form of philanthropy. By 1901, when he gave the grant to New York City, Carnegie expanded his grant program into the broad, worldwide operation which made him stand out from the others and made him unique in the world of philanthropy. By 1911 he institutionalized this method of giving, turning over his money set aside for philanthropy to the Carnegie Corporation of New York. He was president of the Corporation and its goals were his, to improve the standard of living of humanity, particularly the working poor. Andrew Carnegie died of bronchial pneumonia in 1919. The Carnegie Corporation of New York is still in operation, as are 20 other Carnegie foundations and funds.[5]

New York, 12th March 1901.

Dr J.S.Billings,
    Director New York Public Library.

Dear Mr Billings,

    Our conferences upon the needs of Greater New York for Branch Libraries to reach the masses of the people in every district have convinced me of the wisdom of your plans.

    Sixty-five branches strike one at first as a large order, but as other cities have found one necessary for every sixty or seventy thousand of population the number is not excessive.

    You estimate the average cost of these libraries at, say, $80,000 each, being $5,200,000 for all. If New York will furnish sites for these Branches for the special benefit of the masses of the people, as it has done for the Central Library, and also agree in satisfactory form to provide for their main--tenance as built, I should esteem it a rare privilege to be permitted to furnish the money as needed for the buildings, say $5,200,000. Sixty-five libraries at one stroke probably breaks the record, but this is the day of big operations. and New York is sure to be the Very truly yours,

biggest of Cities,

Andrew Carnegie

Carnegie Branch Libraries in the United States and Worldwide

There were just over 2500 Carnegie libraries built in the English speaking countries of the world, at a cost to Andrew Carnegie and the Carnegie Corporation of $56 million. [6] Carnegie gave more than $40 million for over 1680 libraries in the United States in more than 1400 communities. [7] Most of the communities—over 1300—were small towns, and these were particularly favored for donations in the later years of library giving.

Carnegie considered the record New York City grant to be enough of a success to offer Philadelphia $1.5 million three years later, and $1 million to St. Louis soon after. While New York City did not receive money for a central library, 34 cities did receive main buildings along with branches, including Philadelphia and St. Louis. The Carnegie Corporation of New York stopped considering new requests for library grants in 1917 because of the demands of World War I and the shortage of labor and materials. The Corporation resumed support of reading and literacy after the war in 1925, but it changed direction and supported libraries through grants to library schools, university libraries, and librarians' professional associations rather than for building libraries. Despite its change in direction, the Corporation received over 3000 requests for various types of library grants—many for library buildings—from 1917 until the 1960's. [8]

Carnegie's New York City Gift

Andrew Carnegie established residence in New York City in 1867 and lived there part of the time until he died, although he traveled and spent a great deal of time in Scotland. He was a trustee of the New York Free Circulating Library, which merged with The New York Public Library in 1901, and made relatively small donations to the organization at the time. Officials and trustees of the library approached Carnegie more than once but he initially considered New York City to be too rich for his help. By 1901, after the consolidation which created The New York Public Library, he changed his mind as well as his style of giving and offered to fund the branch library network for New York City. This was the year Carnegie sold his business and the beginning of his serious concentration on philanthropy as well as his very large library donations. In fact Carnegie sent the letter to John Shaw Billings offering the $5.2 million the day after the sale of his company became public. John Shaw Billings, nationally respected librarian and Director of The New York Public Library, received most of the credit for persuading Carnegie but Arthur Bostwick, official at The New York Public Library as well as the Brooklyn Public Library, and Mrs. Cross, a New York Free Circulating Library trustee, were also considered instrumental. [9]

Early New York City Libraries

The earliest libraries in New York City were subscription libraries, like the Poppenhusen Institute, school and university libraries, religious libraries, and such special collections as the New-York Historical Society and the American Bar Association. By the second half of the 19th century there were several large free libraries, including the Astor Library, the Lenox Library, the YMCA, the Cooper Union reference reading room, The Pratt Institute library, the Long Island Free Library in Brooklyn, the Long Island City Public Library, and others. Although the New York Free Circulating Library was founded in 1878, branch libraries were scarce, as were free libraries.

Libraries at the Turn of the Nineteenth Century

A great deal of attention was paid to libraries at the turn of the 19th century, as well as other social institutions. At the time of its consolidation in 1898, New York City had a population of about 3 million and was one of the largest cities in the world, second in size only to London when compared to European cities. The population was growing daily, due largely to the massive immigration. Because of the change in society caused by increased urbanization, the

Old Chatham Square Branch, 22 East Broadway, n.d., c. 1903
Chatham Square Carnegie Branch, 33 East Broadway, n.d., c. 1905
Before the Carnegie libraries were built in New York City, branch libraries were not housed in dedicated structures but were frequently located in rented storefronts, like the Chatham Square storefront branch (top), used before the Carnegie was built across the street. (Archives of The New York Public Library Astor, Lenox and Tilden Foundations)

industrial revolution and the great immigration period, wealthy New Yorkers, aware of the dangers of a large, poor, uneducated populace, concentrated on social programs to alleviate some of the miserable conditions. This was a period when model housing, public baths, community centers, and libraries were accepted as necessary for a civilized society. By 1904, 22 states, including New York, had some form of state library commission and library laws allowing for public support of libraries.[10]

By 1900, New York City was well on its way to having one of the major reference libraries in the country. The question was where to get the money for branch libraries. Most library support was private: New York City support, although enabled by state legislation as early as the 1830's, was neither high nor consistent at the turn of the century and was confined to operation and maintenance. New York trailed other states and cities, especially Massachusetts, in library support. New York City ranked ninth in per capita spending on libraries in 1900.[11]

Consolidation of the New York City Libraries

New York City had and still has three separate and distinct library corporations: the Brooklyn Public Library, The New York Public Library and The Queens Borough Public Library. The New York Public Library encompasses the boroughs of the Bronx, Manhattan and Staten Island. This abundance of library institutions reflects the history of New York City, which was not a unified city until 1898 when the five boroughs came together to form what was then known as Greater New York. All three library entities were created at the end of the 19th century from collections of individual free libraries, reference libraries, and subscription libraries. By the time of the Carnegie grant, the library consolidations were nearly complete. The New York Public Library was established in 1895. This was an independent, private corporation which received limited public funding. The board of trustees elected its members, although there were a few ex-officio municipal positions added in 1899 and 1902.[12] The private organization was composed of the Astor and Lenox Libraries and the Tilden Trust and was primarily concerned with building the central reference library on Fifth Avenue, opened in 1911. In 1901 the Manhattan-based New York Free Circulating Library merged with The New York Public Library to provide the beginning of a branch library network. Most of the other small independent libraries merged with The New York Public Library in the early years of the 20th century. A number of these independent libraries were eventually housed in new Carnegie branches, among them the Aguilar, St. Agnes, Washington Heights, Harlem, and Webster Libraries. The New York Public Library, responsible for Manhattan and the Bronx at its inception, added Staten Island at the time of the Carnegie grant.[13]

The Brooklyn Public Library was established by state legislation in 1892, although it did not begin operating until 1897.[14] By 1902, the core of the organization was the formerly private collection of the Brooklyn Library, as well a number of small independent libraries. Several of these, Brownsville, Bedford, Fort Hamilton, Washington Irving, and Flatbush, were later housed in Carnegie branches. The Brooklyn Public Library was an independent corporation but the New York City mayor, comptroller and borough president sat on the board of trustees ex-officio and its employees were in the civil service. After formation, the Brooklyn Public Library expanded additionally through the rental of space, and the rented storefront or first floor was the typical branch library before the Carnegie buildings were built. The branches were critical to the operation of the Brooklyn Public Library, which did not open its large Grand Army Plaza central building until 1941. The library unsuccessfully requested funding in 1901 for a central library from the Carnegie grant.[15]

The foundation of The Queens Borough Public Library was the Long Island City Public Library, which was formed in 1896 from the collection of William Nelson. After the 1898 consolidation of New York City, this library became the Queens Borough Library with responsibility for the whole borough. Several independent libraries merged with this new municipally supported library and three of them, Flushing, Poppenhusen and Richmond Hill, were soon housed in newly constructed Carnegie branch buildings. The original Long Island City building functioned as the central library and held administrative offices until 1906. In 1907 the Queens

Seward Park Branch Library, 192 East Broadway, 1911
The Carnegie branches were sited in conspicuous locations and several, like the Seward Park Branch,
were placed in or adjacent to parks.
(Archives of The New York Public Library Astor, Lenox and Tilden Foundations)

Borough Library was incorporated under the present name, The Queens Borough Public Library. While an independent corporation, its trustees, like Brooklyn, were appointed by the mayor and the staff was in the civil service. After the 1907 incorporation, administrative offices moved between branches until 1930, when a Central Building opened in Jamaica. Since 1968 this building has been occupied by the Queens Family Court, with The Queens Borough Public Library Central Branch now located on Merrick Boulevard in Jamaica.

Agreement Between New York City and Andrew Carnegie

In 1901 an agreement was signed between the City of New York and Andrew Carnegie's selected representatives: The New York Public Library, the Brooklyn Public Library and the Queens Public Library (as it was known at the time). The original agreement called for Andrew Carnegie to furnish funds necessary for building 65 branch libraries estimated at $80,000 each for a total of $5.2 million.[16] The New York Public Library received $3.36 million to be used for 42 branches, the Brooklyn Public Library received $1.6 million for 20 branches, and The Queens Borough Public Library, in that sparsely populated borough, received $240,000 for three branches.[17] In return, New York City promised to provide sites for the libraries, to maintain and repair the buildings and to spend not less that 10% of the grant of $5.2 million each year to do so, to make them free and accessible at all reasonable hours (specified at least from 9AM to 9PM) every day of the week except Sunday but including holidays. This was a major increase in opening hours for the libraries.

Ultimately, several items in the agreement required clarification and resolution. Purchase of the books, a subject which had been at issue in other Carnegie funded libraries, came up in New York City. Carnegie generally required that the local municipality stock the library, but the subject was ambiguous in the agreement. It was decided that New York City would pay for the books and enabling legislation was passed so that bonds could be issued for purchases. Another detail involved the City's maintenance requirements. It was decided that 10% of the grant was the minimum that must be spent and that according to the terms of the agreement it was certainly possible to spend more than that.

Andrew Carnegie's Involvement in Planning

Andrew Carnegie was more involved in the planning of the New York City branch libraries than was usual. In this period of intensive giving after 1900, he professed to want nothing to do with the details of library building after the general principals were agreed upon and nearly always insisted that the municipalities handle all of the details themselves. In New York, however, Carnegie was a member of The New York Public Library board from 1902.[18] He lived near and socialized with the people involved. John S. Billings met frequently with Carnegie to discuss progress. Carnegie kept to his tradition, though, of not attending opening ceremonies. This tradition was based on his philosophy of non-interference with the details of library building and programming but it was undoubtedly reinforced by the prospect of attending nearly 2500 library openings worldwide.

Site Selection

Sites for the Carnegie branches were selected by the libraries with approval by New York City. The New York Public Library's trustees, aided by the administrative staff, kept responsibility for direct oversight of the library construction while the Brooklyn Public Library and The Queens Borough Public Library boards designated specialized Carnegie Committees.[19] This system kept the Carnegie money out of the grasp of Tammany Hall. In fact, the library construction was remarkably free of political cronyism and patronage in a period in the City's history when this was a common occurrence.

115th Street Branch Library, 203 West 115th Street, n.d., c. 1910
Hamilton Grange Branch Library, 503 West 145th Street, n.d., c. 1910
These two branches designed by McKim, Mead & White Architects are among the most formal in style of the Carnegie branches.
(Archives of The New York Public Library Astor, Lenox and Tilden Foundations)

Before individual sites were selected, each of the library administrations developed a plan for branch coverage by charting neighborhoods and current and expected population density. The community and local government officials were consulted. In Staten Island, for example, an advisory group of residents was formed to consult with The New York Public Library Board of Trustees on the location of the branches.[20] The New York Public and Brooklyn Public Libraries chose New York City attorney Alanson T. Briggs to propose sites and to act as agent for the libraries and liaison to New York City while The Queens Borough Public Library Carnegie Committee investigated and selected the sites themselves.[21]

It was in the site acquisition that New York City officials discovered how expensive Andrew Carnegie's grant really was.[22] When the Carnegie grant was accepted by the City, it was hoped by library and City officials that many of the sites would be donated, but almost all were bought by the City, a number through condemnation proceedings. The sites for the Aguilar, Kingsbridge and Poppenhusen, and parts of the sites for Flushing and Tottenville were donated. Far Rockaway was located on a school site owned by the City. The sites were not all vacant lots, and several had buildings on them which had to be cleared. The acquisition of sites was a significant part of the cost of establishing the branch network. The site costs for The New York Public Library, for example, amounted to just under half of the cost of the buildings, over $1.6 million.

While there was no major controversy in the establishment of the branch libraries, site selection was the primary area of discussion. All of the communities in New York City wanted the popular libraries in their immediate neighborhood. There was a great deal of lobbying by property owners for the Carnegie Committee to recommend purchase of the properties. By 1910, due primarily to the costs involved, there were still 12 sites to be acquired at a time when all the branches were expected to have been built. Most of the branches were built by 1915.

The Carnegie branch libraries were meant to stand out as libraries, to be centrally located and, if possible, to be near other civic sites like schools, social service centers, or YM/YWCA's. The philosophy behind the site selection was succinctly expressed in 1901 by George L. Rives, Secretary of The New York Public Library:

> "The Trustees are of the opinion that in establishing branch libraries it is of great importance to establish them, as far as possible, in conspicuous positions on well frequented streets. In some measure the same principles should be applied that would govern in the selection of a site for a retail store. The fact that a branch library is constantly before the eyes of the neighboring residents so that all are familiar with its location will undoubtedly tend to increase its usefulness."[23]

This retail analogy was used again in connection with the design of the buildings, with The New York Public Library trustees requiring that each branch building should advertise itself, with the reading rooms to function as a show window does in a store.[24]

Architects' Committees and Design Guidelines

The libraries were designed by some of the leading architects in New York City as well as in some cases in the country. Nearly all of the architects had designed a major public monument in the City at or before the time of the planning and construction of the Carnegie branches.

The New York Public Library Executive Committee initially appointed a temporary advisory committee on architecture consisting of Charles F. McKim, John M. Carrere and Walter Cook to advise them on how to proceed. The committee advised that the branches be uniform in design, materials, general character and scale and that differing site and size requirements would provide sufficient variety. They recommended forming a committee of architects, from two to five firms, to design the buildings in cooperation with each other and to be directly selected rather than through competitions for reasons of economy and speed. The committee also reported that two or three contractors be selected, for the same reasons.[25]

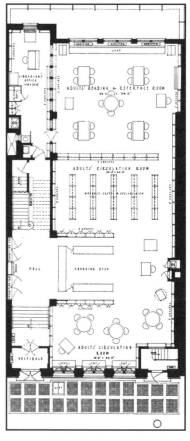

Fort Washington Branch Library,
535-7 West 179th Street
Photograph, n.d., c. 1914 and First Floor Plan, 1914
This Manhattan Carnegie, designed by Cook & Welch
Architects, is typical of the vertically planned,
stone-faced Manhattan branches.
(Archives of The New York Public Library Astor,
Lenox and Tilden Foundations)

On the advice of the temporary committee on architecture, the Executive Committee of The New York Public Library created an Advisory Committee of Architects in 1901, consisting of exactly the same architects as those in the initial architects' advisory committee. All of the committee recommendations were accepted and implemented except for the selection of contractors, who were ultimately selected by competitive bidding.[26]

The Carnegie Committees of the Brooklyn Public Library and The Queens Borough Public Library formed similar architects advisory committees in 1902. The formation of an architects' advisory committee was the most significant event affecting the plan, design and construction of the branch libraries. This method enhanced the image of the branches as a collection of buildings, rather than individual structures in different parts of the City and produced a strong, uniform design concept. The architects' committees agreed on the general plans, the overall style and the materials. The committee also reviewed in detail all of the designs for the libraries and frequently made comments on them. This procedure prefigures the guidelines that were developed in 1911 by James Bertram, Andrew Carnegie's secretary, because so many cities were spending money on elaborate buildings and failing to finish them.

The New York Public Library architects' committee was composed of nationally recognized architects: Charles F. McKim, of McKim, Mead & White, one of the preeminent firms in the country, John M. Carrere, whose firm Carrere & Hastings designed the central library on Fifth Avenue, and Walter Cook, of Babb, Cook & Willard, a major New York firm and architect for Andrew Carnegie. The architects were to collaborate fully with each other and with the library to develop design guidelines and plans. Each firm was to design a library which was to be approved by the rest of the committee. After that, the three architecture firms on the committee were to share the rest of the library commissions. The three firms were to be paid 5% of the total cost of the first building designed, originally estimated at $80,000 per building, 4% for the second and 3.5% for the rest.

After initial agreement, Andrew Carnegie objected in late 1901 to the details of the architects' selection and fees. He did not agree with the percentage fee, which he considered uneconomical and inefficient. He objected to the selection of just three fashionable firms, preferring architectural competitions and a more open procedure. One of the firms on the committee, Babb, Cook & Willard, had just designed the Carnegie family's house on Fifth Avenue, now the Cooper Hewitt National Design Museum. The New York Times weighed in with an objection as well, stating that there would not be enough variety using just three firms.[27] Carnegie was persuaded, however, to go along with the selection process by John Billings, who stated that the trustees believed that the committee system would be faster and cheaper than competitions and would produce more unified results. Billings explained his reasoning in a letter to Carnegie in 1901:

> "But the Trustees believe that the present case, [unlike the central library] where forty odd buildings are to be erected, is not one in which competition would give satisfactory results. Every one of these buildings ought to be of one distinctive and uniform type, so that the most ignorant child going through the streets of the City will at once know a Carnegie Library when he or she sees it."[28]

Carnegie brought up the subject of competitive bidding again in 1915. Most of the libraries were built by that time and competitive bidding was not instituted, but Edward Tilton, library consultant to the Carnegie Corporation, won the commission for the Washington Irving Branch (1923) in Brooklyn.

The Brooklyn Public Library Advisory Commission of Architects consisted of the chairman, J. Monroe Hewlett of Lord & Hewlett, secretary Raymond F. Almirall, William B. Tubby of Tubby & Brother, R. L. Daus, and Richard A. Walker, of Walker & Morris. Columbia University Professor A.D.F. Hamlin was consulting architect to the Brooklyn committee and was influential in developing the architects' employment agreement and design guidelines.[29]

Muhlenberg Branch Library, 209-11 West 23rd Street, n.d., c. 1906
(Archives of The New York Public Library Astor, Lenox and Tilden Foundations)
Eastern Parkway Branch Library, 1044 Eastern Parkway, n.d., c. 1914
(Brooklyn Public Library, Brooklyn Collection)

There was a controversy over the architects' committee selection process when the Brooklyn AIA found out that the Carnegie Committee, itself appointed by the Brooklyn Public Library Board of Trustees, asked for a list of architects who had studied abroad. At this time in the architecture profession this meant studies at the Ecole des Beaux Arts in Paris. The Brooklyn AIA complained that this denigrated American architecture schools. The Carnegie Committee pointed out that one of the members, William Tubby, was not foreign trained and did not change the make-up of the committee.[30]

The Queens Borough Public Library architects' committee was selected by the Carnegie Committee, with Walter L. Bogert in charge. Fourteen architectural firms applied to the Carnegie Committee and three were selected: Lord & Hewlett, Tuthill & Higgins, and Heins & LaFarge.[31] The firm of Lord & Hewlett was also on the Brooklyn Public Library architects' committee.

Architects

All three of The New York Public Library architecture firms for the Carnegie branch libraries were fashionable and nationally influential firms. The architecture firm of Carrere & Hastings was responsible for the largest number of Carnegie branch libraries, designing fourteen of them which opened between 1904 and 1929. The libraries are all part of The New York Public Library system and are located in the Bronx, Manhattan, and Staten Island. The firm was responsible for all of the Carnegie libraries in Staten Island, as well as the design of the Civic Center in that borough. They designed the magnificent Beaux Arts style Central Branch of The New York Public Library on Fifth Avenue in 1898, three years before the Carnegie grant and this building undoubtedly influenced the style of the branches.

The firm of McKim, Mead & White designed twelve of The New York Public Library Carnegie branches in Manhattan and the Bronx which opened between 1903 and 1914. The firm was very influential at this time and also played a major part in the overall design guidelines and choice of classical style. Just before their selection to the Carnegie library architects' committee the firm designed two monumental university libraries, the Low Memorial Library at Columbia University (1897) and the Gould Memorial Library (1900) at the former New York University uptown campus. Their Carnegie libraries, most of which were in Manhattan, are the most formal, faced in stone with lavish use of rustication at the base or, in the case of the 115th Street Branch (1908), on the entire facade. While keeping to the architects' committee's design guidelines, they have the most variation in the design of their facades. The Chatham Square Branch (1903), for example, features the traditional arched ground floor openings but has recessed second and third floors with giant Ionic columns at the facade while the original building of the Schomburg Branch (1905) has rectangular ground floor openings but a monumental window on the upper two stories highlighted by a decorative metal spandrel. Outside Manhattan the firm designed low-scale brick libraries with stone trim similar to those of Carrere & Hastings and Babb, Cook & Willard. The small, one story brick Kingsbridge Branch (1905) in the Bronx is in sharp contrast to the elaborately carved limestone-faced three story Hamilton Grange Branch (1907) in Manhattan.

The firm of Babb, Cook & Willard designed eight Carnegie branches in Manhattan and the Bronx for The New York Public Library which opened between 1905 and 1909. At the time the firm was involved with the planning of the Carnegie branches, they also designed the landmark Andrew Carnegie residence (1899-1903), now the Cooper Hewitt Museum. This firm became Babb, Cook & Welch in 1909, then Cook, Babb & Welch, and then Cook & Welch. Babb Cook & Welch designed one Carnegie branch in 1909 and Cook & Welch designed two in 1913 and 1914. Altogether the variations of the firm designed eleven Carnegie branches. Their libraries, while elegant, have the least variation, with the 67th and 96th Street Branches (1905) almost identical to each other, the St. Agnes and Columbus Branches (1908; 1909) also alike, before the Columbus Branch was altered, and the Webster and West 40th Street Branches (1906; 1913) very similar.

Bedford Branch Library, 496 Franklin Avenue, n.d., c. 1910
Brownsville Branch Library, 61 Glenmore Avenue, n.d. c. 1908
These two Brooklyn Carnegie branches designed by Lord & Hewlett Architects illustrate
the horizontally planned branches in Brooklyn, the Bronx, Queens and Staten Island.
(Brooklyn Public Library, Brooklyn Collection)

Each of the Brooklyn architects on the committee designed four Carnegie branches in that borough. Raymond E. Almirall's libraries are the most formal of the Brooklyn architects. The large Park Slope Branch (1906) is a full seven bays wide with a projecting entrance marked by pairs of Doric columns supporting a carved stone pediment and with a spectacular interior featuring stained glass arched entries and a vaulted stained glass vestibule ceiling. The Eastern Parkway Branch (1914) is the only Brooklyn Carnegie with a limestone facade. The Pacific Branch (1903) has an unusual semi-circular plan and intricate limestone ornament. At the time he was working on the Carnegie branches, he designed the elaborate Beaux Arts style landmark Emigrant Savings Bank (1908-12).

Rudolph L. Daus was a Brooklyn architect who designed two major buildings in Downtown Brooklyn, the grand, Beaux Arts style 1898 Telephone Company Building and the now demolished 1905 Hall of Records. He was a partner in the firm of Daus & Otto from 1909. His Saratoga and Walt Whitman Branches (1908) are very similar, long low brick buildings with projecting entrance bays and unpretentious classical stone trim. His Greenpoint Branch (1906), now demolished, was one of the largest and grandest of the Brooklyn Carnegies.

William Tubby was a respected Brooklyn architect most well-known for public and residential architecture in the Romanesque and Colonial Revival styles. He designed the landmark Pratt Institute Free Library in 1896. His Carnegie libraries, all different from one another but bearing the Carnegie branch characteristics, exhibit pronounced use of stone ornament and brick detailing. His Carroll Gardens (1905) and DeKalb (1905) Branches feature liberal use of classical limestone ornament on three bay red brick facades.

Richard A. Walker of Walker & Morris Architects designed four Carnegie branches as well as the Berkely Institute in Brooklyn and the Ogden Free Library in Walton, New York. His Arlington Branch (1906) has one of the finest branch library interiors in the City. The firm of Walker & Morris dissolved in about 1912 and Richard Walker joined Warren & Wetmore Architects before designing the Red Hook Branch (1915, demolished).

Lord & Hewlett designed Carnegie branches in both Brooklyn and Queens. The two architects worked for McKim, Mead & White before setting up practice on their own. A year after their last Carnegie library opened they participated in the design of the imposing Classical Revival style Brooklyn Masonic Temple in 1909. Three of their seven branches have been demolished, as have three Carrere & Hastings' Carnegie branches. Their Bedford Branch was one of the much praised first five Brooklyn Carnegies.

The architecture firm of Tuthill & Higgins designed two Carnegie branches, both for The Queens Borough Public Library. The Astoria Branch (1904) followed the guidelines the least, with a front entrance topped by a Flemish gable standing alone in its own bay at an angle to the rest of the building. This entrance was altered probably in a 1930's Works Progress Administration (WPA) project. The Richmond Hill Branch (1905), with its original three bay facade with projecting center entrance looked much more like a typical Carnegie branch. The large library has since had a bay added.

Heins & LaFarge, although selected for the Queens committee, designed only the Poppenhusen Branch (1904). The architectural firm was well known for its public buildings, including several landmark subway stations. At the time they designed the Carnegie library, they were also the first architects for the landmark Cathedral Church of St. John the Divine.

There were four other architects of Carnegie branches. The Yorkville Branch (1902) was planned before the Carnegie grant, with James Brown Lord already hired. The architect designed the Bloomingdale Branch for the New York Free Circulating Library in 1898. 32 He followed the architects' committee guidelines, particularly in plan, but his facade is more ornate than the later branches. Herts & Tallant were the designers of the first Aguilar library on the site, when Aguilar was still an independent library, and were hired to design what was apparently not a new branch but rather an extensive renovation.

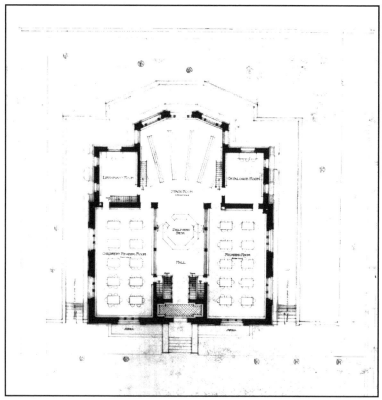

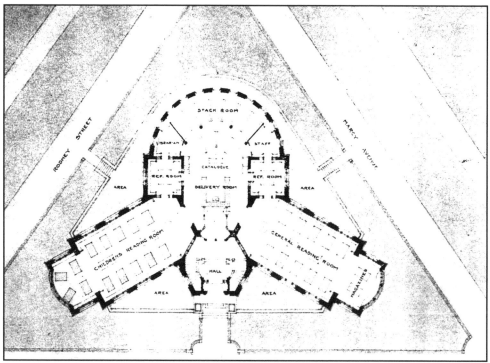

The first of the Brooklyn Carnegie branches were praised for their innovative
plans in the Library Journal in March 1903.
Bedford Branch Library, 496 Franklin Avenue,
Williamsburgh Branch Library, 226-46 Division Avenue,
(Brooklyn Public Library, Brooklyn Collection)

Each of the library systems built libraries in the 1920's with money left over from the original grant. The original procedures had apparently dissolved by this late date and new architects were hired in Brooklyn and Queens. Edward Tilton, a Carnegie Corporation library consultant who, with Alciphron Boring, designed the Ellis Island complex in 1897, was the architect for the Brooklyn Public Library's Tudor Revival style Washington Irving Branch (1923). Robert F. Schirmer designed the Woodhaven Branch in 1924. He was also responsible for The Queens Borough Public Library 1927-8 Central Branch in Jamaica. The New York Public Library continued to retain committee architects for their branch libraries. McKim, Mead & White designed the Fordham Branch in 1923 and Carrere & Hastings designed the Hunt's Point Branch in 1929.

Library Plans

The librarians had a major say in the designs, in particular the plans. They met with the architects initially and commented on the plans after they were drawn up. It is probable that Andrew Carnegie influenced this procedure; it was in accordance with his strong belief in the trained, professional librarian and in economical and efficient library buildings and plans. For example, while The New York Public Library architects would have preferred center entrances on their classical style buildings the librarians wanted side entrances to maximize the space and natural light for the reading rooms. Librarians were dissatisfied with 19th century libraries, which they considered inefficient and uncomfortable. There were closed stacks and the librarian retrieved all of the books. The two-tiered stacks were difficult to climb, and time-consuming to retrieve books. In order for the lower part of the library to be comfortable, the top tier was generally too hot for the safety of the books as well as the comfort of the librarians. The characteristic reading alcoves were not possible to oversee from one central place and they were far from the librarian's desk.[33]

The Carnegie plans, developed by the architects committee with a great deal of participation by the librarians, incorporated the progressive library thinking of the period, where stacks were easily accessible to librarians, and light, airy reading rooms were provided. The use of the central charge desk was another modern library idea. Some new plan types were developed, including the unusual semi-circular plan of the Williamsburgh and Pacific Branches, featured in the 1903 *Library Journal.* The influential professional magazine called the plans of the Williamsburgh and the Bedford Branches (a rectangular plan) representatives of "perhaps the most interesting and satisfactory type of branch library building yet evolved."[34]

Style

There was no question that the style of the libraries would be classical. This, and especially Beaux Arts, was the recognized style for public buildings for this period. The early 20th century was the height of the City Beautiful movement. The influence of The New York Public Library's monumental Beaux Arts main branch as well as the major architectural influence of the 1893 World's Columbian Exposition in Chicago and the subsequent City Beautiful movement made the use of the classical style inevitable. A moderating influence was Andrew Carnegie who stressed simple, modest buildings. By the standard of public buildings of the period, these libraries were not overly ornate, especially on the interior. The buildings, in particular the freestanding libraries outside of Manhattan, shared characteristics with the other Carnegie libraries in the United States, notably their size, proportions, use of classical ornament, and overall plan.

Design Features of the Collection

In the early 20th century there was a clear progression of library architecture by type and borough. Carrere & Hastings' Central Branch on Fifth Avenue (1898-1911) is one of the most elaborate and formal buildings in New York City. The Manhattan Carnegie branches, intended

MAJOR CHARACTERISTICS
CARNEGIE LIBRARIES
OF NEW YORK CITY

Exterior

❏ Separate and distinct structure of masonry construction with red brick or limestone facade

❏ Prominent entrance reached by a flight of stone steps and flanked by lampposts or lanterns

❏ Classical style - Beaux Arts or Classical Revival

❏ Classical ornament - columns, pilasters, pediments, cornices, quoins, keystones

❏ Liberal use of limestone for entire facade or for trim

❏ Large windows with wooden, multi-paned sash filling the opening from top to bottom, and set in slightly from the plane of the facade, creating a shadowed effect

❏ Flat or low hipped roof

Interior

❏ Open, high-ceilinged space lit by abundant natural light

❏ Separate vestibule leading to main reading area

❏ Plaster ceilings, simple in design, sometimes with cove molding or plaster beams

❏ Plaster columns, round or rectangular, with simple molded capitals and bases

❏ Prominent wooden charge desk

❏ Simple wooden window trim, molded baseboards, wood wainscoting

❏ Wooden book shelves at perimeter and used as room dividers

❏ Numerous reading tables in the reading rooms

to be the souls of simplicity, were nevertheless built with elegant limestone facades, discrete but ornate stone carving and rustication, tall arched doors and windows, pronounced classical limestone cornices. The branch libraries in the Bronx, Brooklyn, Staten Island and Queens were less formal and ornate, with brick and stone facades standing one or two stories tall.

The Carnegie branches share many broad architectural features and these features define the character of the libraries as well as identifying them as New York City Carnegie branch libraries. These features are common to most, but not necessarily all, of the Carnegie libraries. The collection of libraries can be divided into two general categories, the attached mid-block Manhattan branches and the freestanding branches in the Bronx, Brooklyn, Staten Island and Queens. The attached branches are generally faced in limestone, three stories high and three bays wide with tall arched entrances in one of the two side bays. They are located in mid-block with buildings on both sides and are built to the building line. The freestanding branches are all located on corner sites, frequently with land around them enclosed by a wrought iron fence. They are primarily two stories high and three or five bays wide, with entrances in the center bay and windows on all sides.

All of the Carnegie branch libraries are separate and distinct structures. They are of solid, fireproof masonry construction with a red brick or limestone facade and limestone trim.[35] Most of the limestone was a light-colored Indiana limestone. There is liberal use of limestone, for the entire facade or for trim, and frequent use of rustication in Manhattan libraries. There are Maine granite bases and granite, marble, or limestone steps.

The branches are nearly all designed in a classical style, Beaux Arts, Classical or Renaissance Revival. There is classically-inspired ornament on the exterior: columns, pilasters, pediments, cornices, quoins, keystones, and other embellishments. The large windows take a fairly high percentage of the facade for a classical masonry building. The original window sash was wood, with windows multi-paned and set in slightly from the plane of the facade, creating a shadowed effect. The window sash fills the masonry opening from top to bottom. There is stone trim around the door and windows, and a number of facades feature classical pediments. There is a frequent use of arched openings. The buildings are topped by a classical stone or sheet metal cornice. The roofs are flat or have a low hip shape and most libraries had skylights. The roofing material varied, with tar felt and gravel being used most frequently on the flat roofs, and flat or Spanish tile on the hipped roofs. Standing seam metal roofing was also used, for main roofs with a pitch and for towers or other projections.

All of the Carnegie branches have a prominent entrance reached by a flight of steps in the center of the facade or to one side of the facade. There is a tall door opening, trimmed with stone, often topped by a pediment, with a decorative glass transom. There are exterior lamp posts flanking the doorway, or lanterns in Manhattan.

On the interior, there are high plaster ceilings, with modest plaster ornament like cove molding. There are large round or rectangular columns with molded bases and capitals. The buildings are entered generally by a one bay wide vestibule, often with wood paneling, leading to main reading area which is raised up a flight of steps. Originally there was a centrally located wooden charge desk, most frequently made of oak. In the more horizontal plans outside of Manhattan, reading rooms are located on either side of the charge desk. There was frequent use of reading nooks with fireplaces. In the compact, vertical Manhattan branches reading rooms are located on separate floors and there are prominent side stairs with decorative iron railings. Relatively simple wooden window trim, molded baseboards, and some wood wainscoting can be found in most branches. There are multiple sets of reading tables in the reading rooms. Most of the libraries have bronze plaques with a bust of Andrew Carnegie, the name of the library, architect and date of opening. They have nearly all been moved from the exterior to the interior and can often be found on a wall in the entrance vestibule.

The lighting and shelving systems shared similar characteristics in all of the Carnegie branches. Original book stacks were wood or metal. Wooden perimeter shelving was located below window level and freestanding four to five foot wooden book cases acted as room dividers. A

DeKalb Branch Library, 784 Bushwick Avenue, n.d., c. 1905
(Brooklyn Public Library, Brooklyn Collection)
58th Street Branch Library, Demolished, 121-7 East 58th Street, n.d. c. 1910
Schavendorf Photographer
(Archives of The New York Public Library Astor, Lenox and Tilden Foundations)

large percentage of the original shelving has been replaced but some of these stacks and perimeter cases can still be found. Original double-tiered book stacks with glass panel flooring at the mezzanine level can be seen at several branches, including the Pacific Branch in Brooklyn. The original electric lighting consisted of glass and metal pendant fixtures as well as table lamps. Few original light fixtures have survived later 20th century renovations and the Carnegies currently have a wide variety of fluorescent and incandescent lighting.

Construction of the Carnegie Branches

The construction of the branches spanned a 27 year period, the last libraries being built after Andrew Carnegie died in 1919. There were 67 branches opened from 1902 to 1929. Of these structures, 57 buildings are still standing and 54 are operating libraries today. Of the three branches not operating as libraries, all have maintained a public use. The former Rivington Branch is the Chinese Nazarene Church, the former West 40th Street Branch is part of Covenant House, a drug rehabilitation center, and the former Kingsbridge Branch is the Spuyten Duyvil Infantry and Preschool, a nursery school.

Of the ten demolished branches, seven were replaced by new branches on the same site: Greenpoint, Red Hook, South (now Sunset Park), High Bridge, 58th Street, Flushing, and Far Rockaway. The current Hamilton Fish Branch is a few blocks away from the former Carnegie branch site, which is now part of highrise public housing. The current Riverside and Kingsbridge Branches are also near the former Carnegie branch sites. The former St. Gabriel's Branch is part of the approach to the Midtown Tunnel.

CURRENT BRANCHES

	Built	Extant	Operating
Brooklyn Public Library:	21	18	18
The New York Public Library:	39	34	31
(Bronx)	(9)	(8)	(7)
(Manhattan)	(26)	(22)	(20)
(Staten Island)	(4)	(4)	(4)
The Queens Borough Public Library:	7	5	5
Total:	67	57	54

The first branch to open as a Carnegie library was Yorkville in Manhattan in 1902. This library was planned before the Carnegie grant and was selected to be a Carnegie branch before construction. The first branch library opened which was planned after the Carnegie grant was the Pacific Branch in Brooklyn in 1903, but the first Carnegie building begun was the Williamsburgh Branch. This was accompanied by a major cornerstone laying ceremony in 1903, with the Mayor, Seth Low, and hundreds of onlookers participating. While not as grand as this one, all of the opening ceremonies for the Carnegie branches included celebrations, speeches by government and library officials, and frequently hundreds of people from the community in attendance.

The first few years after the grant were spent planning, selecting sites and discussing the terms of the agreement. Newspapers as well as Carnegie himself started commenting on the slow rate at which the libraries were being built.[36] The pace picked up, though, and 33 branches were built in 1905 and 1906 alone, bringing the total at the end of 1906 to 42, which was almost two-

Williamsburgh Branch Library, 226-46 Division Avenue, Cornerstone Laying Ceremony, 1903
(Brooklyn Public Library, Brooklyn Collection)

thirds of the libraries ultimately constructed. Indeed, most of the branches—55—were built in the eight years from 1902 to 1909 and this short time span is accounts in part for the dynamic architectural and cultural connections between the buildings.

Changes Over the Years

Although remarkably intact, the Carnegie libraries were altered over the years. Carnegie grant funds were even used for some early alterations at The New York Public Library's Hudson Park and Tremont Branches. There were individual renovations over the years as well as entire organized library campaigns. There were renovations using Civil Works Administration funds in the 1930's at most of the branches of The Queens Borough Public Library and at the Flatbush Branch of the Brooklyn Public Library. Murals funded by the WPA in the 1930's and painted at the Astoria and Richmond Hill Branches still exist today while the Pacific and Brownsville Branch WPA murals have vanished. In the 1940's The New York Public Library installed new lighting in most of the branches and many of the Brooklyn Public Library renovations took place in the 1950's. Most branches have been renovated to one degree or another more than once. Common alterations include replaced doors and windows, new roofing, covered over skylights, overlaid interior finishes such as flooring, replaced lighting fixtures, book stacks and furniture, and modernized mechanical systems.

Programming

The branch libraries provided amenities sadly lacking in the neighborhoods in which they were located. They offered books and periodicals in more than one language, a clean and well-lighted place for reading, programs supporting reading for adults and children, educational lectures, theater, and, perhaps most overlooked, an educated and available staff of librarians for multi-lingual programming from their inception.

The library field and profession crystallized in the latter half of the 19th century, developing a structure and organization. The American Library Association was formed in 1876 and the first library school was established at Columbia University in 1884. Andrew Carnegie was a major benefactor of library schools and training.[37] The newly professional librarians staffing the branches, mostly women, were responsible for the details of the programming at the branches. They acquired, for example, artwork for the walls of the branches for the education of the people using the branches.

The branches were meant to serve all New Yorkers, in particular the growing immigrant population. Foreign language books, newspapers and lectures were common.[38] The languages featured were those most prevalent in the neighborhood. When the Hudson Park Branch opened in Greenwich Village in 1906, it stocked ten thousand books, magazines and newspapers in French, German and English.[39] The Chatham Square Branch stocked books in German, French, Italian, Spanish, Russian, Yiddish, Greek, Arabic, and Chinese.[40] The Tompkins Square Library served the Hungarian immigrant community. Arthur Bostwick described this library as standing out from among the dark tenements and providing "a place where books are given out and where men, women, and children may come to read where it is bright and light and clean."[41] The libraries were tremendously crowded when they opened, serving the community in exactly the way they were intended.

The childrens' reading rooms and programs were modern ideas not cultivated in the old subscription libraries or the reference libraries and were innovative features of the Carnegie branch libraries of the early 20th century. The New York Public Library's childrens' reading programs were highlighted in the 1911 Child Welfare Exhibit, a social reform event held at the now demolished 71st Regiment Armory in Manhattan. The library set up a booth at the exhibit and hired Lewis Hine to photograph children in the branches, which were displayed at the exhibit. Some of these photos are printed for the first time in this publication today.[42]
In addition to foreign language and children's programs, most of the libraries had an auditorium

Tottenville Branch Library, 7430 Amboy Road, 1991 Elevation
Stephen D. Weinstein/John Ellis & Associates Joint Venture Architects
Tompkins Square Branch Library, 331 East 10th Street, 1992
Sketch by Saija Singer, Cooper Union '96

for community events and programs. This was the subject of a debate when the branches were being built. Some librarians wanted the branches to have strictly traditional library functions, with stacks and reading rooms only. Other social reformers of the period wanted the branches to be one-stop-shopping community centers, with community rooms, recreational facilities, and even baths. All of this was not possible for both budgetary reasons and because of the objections of librarians who did not want the purpose of the libraries diluted, but some libraries were placed near community centers, YMCA's or social service organizations and many branches incorporated a community room or auditorium. The Hudson Park Branch, for example, is located next to a community center and pool, the Seward Park Branch is across the street from a social services institution, and the Williamsburgh Branch is located adjacent to a YMCA. Possibly as many as half of the libraries were located near schools.

Carnegie Libraries Today

The Carnegie libraries today make up one quarter of the entire library system in New York City. The collection of 54 operating Carnegie libraries in the five boroughs represents one of the earliest public/private partnerships. The libraries are still major educational, intellectual and social centers in their communities. Programs popular when the libraries were built, such as childrens' reading and foreign language programs continue to have great significance while computers and new book display techniques have arisen to ensure that the libraries will continue to be beneficial to the neighborhoods. After nearly a century the buildings and sites still function as worthwhile circulating libraries. The well-designed functional spaces are demonstrably adaptable to modern technology and to programming needs of the future.

The public commitment to the Carnegies today is evident in their official recognition as landmarks—five Carnegie branches are designated individual New York City landmarks and two are located in historic districts—and in the appropriation of public funds for construction and programming. In the next five years, the City will manage capital improvements costing approximately $20 million to more than half of the Carnegie branches. While these buildings are remarkably intact, they have been and continue to be the subject of restoration and rehabilitation. Heating, ventilation, air conditioning and electrical systems have been improved and upgraded, lighting is being restored in some cases, book stacks have been rehabilitated and replaced, and windows have been repaired. Handicapped accessibility is being addressed through the addition of elevators, ramps, and widened doors.

The City, in conjunction with the Brooklyn Public Library, The New York Public Library, and The Queens Borough Public Library, has expanded its attention to the Carnegies by developing a capital program that balances the preservation of the nearly 100 year old buildings with contemporary architectural and programmatic requirements. The challenge today for administrators, designers, and preservationists is to maintain the architectural and historical character of the Carnegies while incorporating improved access and modern equipment into the structures. There are a number of issues to be addressed in the pursuit of balance between preservation and modernization: the preservation of the original exterior design and such historic fabric as signage, landscape, doors, and windows while making the branches accessible to everyone, improving security, and enhancing energy efficiency; retaining the historic plan, fabric, and character of the interior while restoring and improving lighting, inserting computer systems, and upgrading the mechanical infrastructure. The following selected projects illustrate the capital improvement program, demonstrating the range of scope and complexity of the projects. This group represents a small percentage of the work planned and in progress.

The New York Public Library is composed of 83 branch libraries in the boroughs of the Bronx, Manhattan, and Staten Island, 31 of which are Carnegies. In the Bronx, the Mott Haven Branch (1905) is slated for an exterior restoration which not only respects the original design and materials, but also restores them where necessary. Located in the Mott Haven Historic District, the landmark library was designed by Carrere & Hastings. In 1995 Cabrerra Barricklo Architects completed plans for a new roof, restoration of the wood windows, and masonry repointing, repair and cleaning. Interior renovation costing $480,000 is planned, with the

Flatbush Branch Library, Interior, n.d., c. 1905
22 Linden Boulevard
Fort Hamilton Branch Library, Interior, n.d., c. 1907
Fourth Avenue at 95th Street
(Brooklyn Public Library, Brooklyn Collection)

design phase scheduled to begin in 1996. A recent plan by DCI International Architects to make the Morrisania Branch (1908, Babb, Cook & Willard), accessible for everyone won an Art Commission Award for design excellence.

In Manhattan, the 96th Street Branch (1905), designed by Babb, Cook & Willard, was renovated as part of an ongoing project by Samuel J. De Santo and Associates, Architects with particular sympathy for the original interior features. Elements characteristic of the Carnegies, including high plaster ceilings, rectangular plaster columns, an interior staircase with a decorative iron rail, and an oak paneled screen were retained. The interior was painted in a palette of colors sympathetic to the original period color scheme. This renovation, begun in 1986, is an example of a successful public/private partnership, with three-quarters of the funds raised from private sources and one-quarter from the City.

The Manhattan Tompkins Square Branch (1904) is another example of public/private funding of revnovations. Originally designed by McKim, Mead & White, the building is undergoing renovation by Rothzeid Kaiserman Thomson and Bee Associates. The library is part of The New York Public Library's Adopt-A-Branch program.

The Tottenville Branch (1904) in Staten Island was designed by Carrere & Hastings Architects and was one of the first ten Carnegie branches opened. It was restored in 1993. The design and historic feeling of the library were retained by the architects John Ellis and Stephen Weinstein. The brick and limestone exterior was cleaned and repaired and the handicapped access ramp was innovatively incorporated into the park-like landscape. A new air conditioning and electrical system was integrated into the building with sensitivity to the original fabric. The original millwork was retained or replicated and the large chandeliers, lost in a previous rehabilitation, were recreated from an old postcard photograph. The original building cost $27,000; the restoration cost just over $1 million. The restoration won an Art Commission Award for Design Excellence in 1991, the 1994 Municipal Art Society's fifth annual New York Preservation Award, and the 1995 Preservation League of Staten Island Award.

Plans for the Stapleton Branch (1907, Carrere & Hastings) in Staten Island include installation of a new roof and restoration of deteriorated eaves, accessibility improvements on the exterior and interior, and other interior work. The architects for the over $1 million project are Ehrenkrantz & Eckstut Architects.

The Brooklyn Public Library is composed of 59 branches, 18 of which are Carnegies. The Flatbush Branch (1905), designed by R. L. Daus, was completely renovated in a 1937 WPA project and now looks like a Carnegie library that was built in the 1930's. Handicapped accessibility is one of the major aspects of the general renovation project by Margaret Helfand Architects. The main floor reading room for Flatbush, like most of the Carnegies in all of the boroughs, is reached by a steep flight of steps and designing architecturally sympathetic access for the disabled a challenging task. In addition, some important original elements removed in the 1960's will be replaced.

Seven Carnegie libraries in Brooklyn are included in a $1.2 million project to renovate the buildings for handicapped access, to comply with the Americans for Disabilities Act (ADA). Special attention will be paid by Kupiec Koutsomitis Architects PC to retain the original and characteristic features which make the Carnegie branches unique. The branches, Arlington, Brownsville, Bushwick, Eastern Parkway, Fort Hamilton, Macon, and Washington Irving, are located on landscaped sites with lawns, most on corners. The design challenge will be to improve access while retaining the character of the individual landscape as well as the architecture.

The Queens Borough Public Library is composed of 62 circulating branches, five of which are Carnegies. The Elmhurst Branch (1906), designed by Lord & Hewlett, is the subject of a current rehabilitation project where the classical elegance is being restored by bringing back the original style doors and windows. In addition, access to the library will be enhanced.

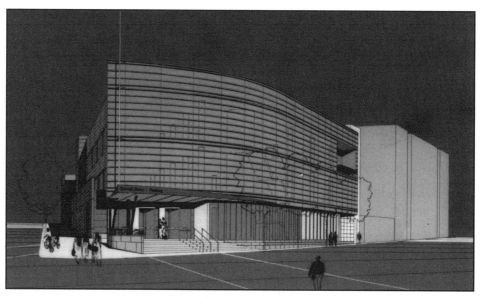

Poppenhusen Branch Library, 121-13 14th Street, n.d., c. 1904
(The Queens Borough Public Library - Long Island Collection);
New Flushing Branch Library on the site of the original Carnegie Library which burned down, 1994 Elevation,
James Stewart Polshek & Associates

The Queens Poppenhusen Branch (1904), designed by Heins & LaFarge, is to be renovated to improve accessibility for ADA compliance. In addition, a new roof will be installed, mechanical systems will be improved and new lighting fixtures will be introduced.

As we approach the centennial celebrations of the first of the over 2500 Carnegie branches in the world, we can acknowledge the foresight of Andrew Carnegie and his record-setting donation to New York City as well as the efforts of The New York Public, Brooklyn Public and The Queens Borough Public Libraries, the Department of General Services, the Mayors, Borough Presidents, City Council members and the generations of citizens to maintain and preserve this great library collection. The Carnegie branch libraries are a valuable and significant resource for our City today, as essential for maintaining a literate and educated populace today as they were nearly one hundred years ago. These remarkably intact libraries richly deserve respectful rehabilitation in time for their centennials. It is hoped that *The Architecture of Literacy* will serve to inform the public as well as to enlighten the administrators, designers and property managers who have stewardship of these irreplaceable libraries.

Harlem Branch Library, Interior, c. 1910, Lewis Hine Photographer
(Archives of The New York Public Library Astor, Lenox and Tilden Foundations).

FOOTNOTES

1. As quoted in George Bobinsky, *Carnegie Libraries* (Chicago: American Library Association, 1969) p. 10.

2. Ibid., p. 11-12.

3. Ibid., p. 11.

4. Ibid., p. 7.

5. Ibid., p.13.

6. Rub, Timothy, "'The Day of Big Operations': Andrew Carnegie and His Libraries," *Architectural Record*: July, 1985.

7. George Bobinsky, "Carnegie Libraries: Their Current and Future Status - the Results of a Survey," *Public Libraries*: January/February, 1991, p. 18-22.

8. Bobinsky, *Carnegie Libraries*, p. 159, 196.

9. Phyllis Dain, *The New York Public Library* (New York: New York Public Library, 1972) p. 210-11.

10. Bobinsky, *Carnegie Libraries*, p. 9.

11. Dain, p. 22-3.

12. Ibid., p. 78-9.

13. Ibid., p. 223; 232-3.

14. Margaret B. Freeman, *The Brooklyn Public Library: A History* (New York, 1966) p. 48. The history of the Brooklyn Public Library, drastically simplified in this essay, has been written about in other publications, including the one mentioned above.

15. Letter from John S. Billings to Frank Hill, 8/5/1901, Brooklyn Public Library Carnegie Correspondence Files.

16. The following year in 1902 the estimated cost of some of the branches was lowered and the number of branches to be built by the NYPL was increased to 'up to fifty.' The total number quoted varied but it appeared to be up to a maximum of seventy-three. The $5.2 million amount of the grant stayed the same. Because of the rising costs over the years, the number of libraries actually built was just two more than sixty-five. The NYPL ended up building thirty-nine branches, three less than the first agreement and eleven less than the hoped-for fifty of the 1902 supplemental agreement. The excess branches came from Brooklyn, which built one more than the original agreement and Queens, which built four extra. The two agreements are summarized in John Cadwalader, Memorandum, 5/1/1911, in NYPL Archives, RG6, Box 10.

17. This allocation was not easily arrived at and there was a great deal of lobbying and discussion about the amounts.

Hudson Park Branch Library
66 Leroy Street
Sketch by Saija Singer, Cooper Union '96

18. *New York Times*, 1/9/1902, 16-9.

19.   In Brooklyn, the Carnegie Committee consisted of four members of the BPL Board of Directors: R. Ross Appleton; John W. Devoy; D.W. McWilliams; David A. Boody. Frank P. Hill, Chief Librarian, acted as clerk of the committee. In Queens the Carnegie Committee consisted of Walter G. Frey, Walter L. Bogert, and Philip Frank. Walter Frey was President of the library and the other two were trustees of the library. In both Brooklyn and Queens, the individuals in the Carnegie Committees were approved by Andrew Carnegie.

20.   Dain, p. 237.

21.   Briggs landed in the middle of a dispute between the NYPL and the City over the slow acquisition of sites - just 32 in ten years rather than the expected 42 in five years - and his contract was terminated in 1910. Dain, p. 243.

22.   In 1904, Comptroller Grout complained about the cost of books and land and stated that he would hesitate to vote for the Carnegie grant if it came up today. (*New York Times* 10/11/1904, 16-4) Comptroller Herman Metz complained of the cost to the City of Carnegies calling it "gold brick philanthropy." In 1908, an advisory committee calculated the costs of the Carnegie branches, not counting site acquisition, as equal to the income on a capital investment of $23.86 million. By 1910, due primarily to the costs involved, there were still 12 sites to be acquired at a time when all the branches were supposed to have been built.   Dain, p. 241-3; *New York Times*, 7/7/1906, 14-6.

23.   NYPL Executive Committee Minutes as quoted in Dain, p. 237.

24.   "Among the conditions imposed by the trustees, there was one which was somewhat of a surprise to the architects, and which was a controlling factor in their designs. This was the requirement that every library building should advertise itself as such, by having a reading room near enough to the sidewalk level for passers by to look as it were into a show window and see the readers." May 12, 1904 Address by Walter Cook to the New York Library Club as quoted in Theodore Wesley Koch, *A Book of Carnegie Libraries* (White Plains, NY: The H.W. Wilson Company, 1917), p. 37.

25.   Report of Committee (Charles McKim, Walter Cook, John Carrere) "Carnegie Library Buildings" 9/30/1901, NYPL Archives, RG5, Box 6; Dain, p. 235-6, Koch, p. 34-41.

26.   Builders were chosen by competitive bidding, although several builders worked on more than one Carnegie branch and just over twenty-six contractors built the sixty-seven branches. Carrere & Hastings used the E.E. Paul Company for seven of their libraries and McKim, Mead & White used the Michael Reid Company for nine of their libraries. The architects worked with this company on several other projects as well. Please see the Builder's List in the Appendix of this publication.

27.   "The Carnegie Libraries," *New York Times* 10/17/1901, 8-3.

28.   Letter to Andrew Carnegie from John S. Billings, 11/9/1901 in NYPL Archives. This idea was also expressed in a press release by George Rives, Secretary of the NYPL, printed in *New York Times* 10/17/1901, 16-2. "The Trustees think that it should be possible for every one to recognize each of these buildings immediately as a branch of the great system of circulating libraries which Mr. Carnegie has planned, and which the city will maintain."

29.   Known as the Advisory Commission of Architects, Brooklyn Public Library Archives Correspondence Files "Carnegie Committee".

30. Brooklyn Times, 5/20/1903; *Tribune* 5/21/1903; *Brooklyn Eagle* 5/26/1903; *New York World*, in Brooklyn Public Library Scrapbooks. The Carnegie Committees were extremely independent and did not generally change plans or actions because of criticism from the press or

from public officials.

31. "Architects Selected for Queens Library," *Flushing Journal*, 3/8/1902.

32. This landmark building, also known as the Ukrainian Academy of Arts and Sciences, is located at 206 West 100th Street.

33. These insights come from the excellent discussion on library plans and the Carnegies in Abigail A. Van Slyck, "'The Utmost Amount of Effectiv [sic] Accommodation': Andrew Carnegie and the Reform of the American Library," *Journal of the Society of Architectural Historian*s: L, #4, December 1991, p. 359-383.

34. *The Library Journal*: 28, #3, March, 1903, p. 103.

35. The specifications for the Manhattan libraries called for Carnegie steel or equivalent (NYPL Archives).

36. Brooklyn Public Library Scrapbooks and Carnegie Correspondence File.

37. Bobinsky, *Carnegie Libraries*, p. 8-9.

38. At The New York Public Library there was a specific book selection process. The librarians met weekly with Mr. Bostwick of the George Bruce Library and chairman of the book selection committee. A list was made of books wanted as well as of standard works and references. The librarians at the meeting would decide which books were most suitable for which circulating library. The final selection was made by John S. Billings. In an article on book selection, the *New York Times* (10/19/1902, 25-3) noted that "When a Carnegie library is established near a settlement of Italians those books dear to the hearts of the sons of Italy will be kept in most numbers on the shelves." The article also noted, though, that "French novels of a certain kind were seldom purchased."
Stocking branch libraries with a percentage of foreign language publications was a relatively new idea not yet fully accepted at the time. There were letters to the editor of the *New York Times* (1/24/1903) demanding to know why tax dollars should be spent to buy books in a foreign language. In a reply which is reminiscent of the current debate on foreign language programs in public schools, Edwin White Gaillard, librarian of the Webster Free Library, stated that libraries were not for individuals but rather for the community, that the city should do everything in its power to raise the intellectual level of its citizens, and that the children of these non-English speakers are "being turned into Americans by the wonderful work of the public schools. It is no less the duty of the public library to endeavor to enlighten the parents" (*New York Times* 1/31/1903, 10-3).

39. Koch, p. 52.

40. "Library for Chinese Opened Downtown," *New York Times* 3/26/1911, 7-7.

41. Koch, p. 54.

42. Robert Sink, "Children in the Library: Lewis Hine's Photographs for the Child Welfare Exhibit of 1911," *Biblion*: I, #2, Spring, 1993.

CATALOGUE OF THE ORIGINAL NEW YORK CITY CARNEGIE LIBRARIES

THE CARNEGIE LIBRARIES OF NEW YORK CITY

BROOKLYN PUBLIC LIBRARY

Arlington Branch Library
203 Arlington Avenue
Opened November 7, 1906
Richard A. Walker/
Walker & Morris, Architects

Bedford Branch Library
496 Franklin Avenue
Opened February 4, 1905
Lord & Hewlett, Architects

Brownsville Branch Library
61 Glenmore Avenue
Opened December 19, 1908
Lord & Hewlett, Architects

Bushwick Branch Library
340 Bushwick Avenue
Opened December 16, 1908
Raymond F. Almirall, Architect

Carroll Gardens Branch Library
396 Clinton Street
Opened March 3, 1905
William B. Tubby, Architect

DeKalb Branch Library
784 Bushwick Avenue
Opened February 11, 1905
William B. Tubby, Architect

Eastern Parkway Branch Library
1044 Eastern Parkway
Opened July 7, 1914
Raymond F. Almirall, Architect

Flatbush Branch Library
22 Linden Boulevard
Opened October 7, 1905
R. L. Daus, Architect

Fort Hamilton Branch Library
Fourth Avenue & 95th Street
Opened October 7, 1907
Lord & Hewlett, Architects

Greenpoint Branch**
107 Norman Avenue
Opened April 7, 1906
R. L. Daus, Architect

Leonard Branch Library
81 Devoe Street
Opened December 1, 1908
William B. Tubby, Architect

Macon Branch Library
361 Lewis Avenue
Opened July 15, 1907
Richard A. Walker/
Walker & Morris, Architects

Pacific Branch Library
25 Fourth Avenue
Opened October 8, 1903
Raymond F. Almirall, Architect

Park Slope Branch Library
431 Sixth Avenue
Opened July 30, 1906
Raymond F. Almirall, Architect

Red Hook Branch**
Visitation Place & Richard Street
Opened April 22, 1915
Richard A. Walker, Architect

Saratoga Branch Library
8 Hopkinson Avenue
Opened September 3, 1908
R.L. Daus/Daus & Otto, Architects

South Branch**
Fourth Avenue & 51st Street
Opened December 9, 1905
Lord & Hewlett, Architects

Continued

* *Decommissioned*
** *Decommissoned and No Longer Standing*

Stone Avenue Branch Library
581 Stone Avenue
Opened September 24, 1914
William B. Tubby, Architect

Walt Whitman Branch Library
St. Edwards Street & Auburn Place
Opened September 1, 1908
R.L. Daus/Daus & Otto, Architects

Washington Irving Branch Library
360 Irving Avenue
Opened May 16, 1923
Edward L. Tilton, Architect

Williamsburgh Branch Library
226-46 Division Avenue
Opened January 28, 1905
Richard A. Walker/Walker & Morris, Architects

THE NEW YORK PUBLIC LIBRARY
THE BRONX

Fordham Branch Borough Library Center
2556 Bainbridge Avenue
Opened September 22, 1923
McKim, Mead & White, Architects

High Bridge Branch**
78 West 168th Street
Opened July 22, 1908
Carrere & Hastings, Architects

Hunt's Point Branch Regional Library
877 Southern Boulevard
Opened July 1, 1929
Carrere & Hastings, Architects

Kingsbridge Branch*
3041 Kingsbridge Avenue
Opened May 19, 1905
McKim, Mead & White, Architects

Melrose Branch Library
910 Morris Avenue
Opened January 14, 1914
Carrere & Hastings, Architects

Morrisania Branch Library
610 East 169th Street
Opened December 1, 1908
Babb, Cook & Willard, Architects

Mott Haven Branch Library
321 East 140th Street
Opened March 31, 1905
Babb, Cook & Willard, Architects

Tremont Branch Library
1866 Washington Avenue
Opened July 22, 1905
Carrere & Hastings, Architects

Woodstock Branch Library
761 East 160th Street
Opened February 17, 1914
McKim, Mead & White, Architects

THE NEW YORK PUBLIC LIBRARY
MANHATTAN

Aguilar Branch Library
172-4 East 110th Street
Opened November 29, 1905
Herts & Tallant, Architects

Chatham Square Branch Regional Library
33 East Broadway
Opened November 2, 1903
McKim, Mead & White, Architects

Columbus Branch Library
742 Tenth Avenue
Opened September 24, 1909
Babb, Cook & Willard, Architects

Epiphany Branch Library
228-30 East 23rd Street
Opened September 20, 1907
Carrere & Hastings, Architects

58th Street Branch**
121-7 East 58th Street
Opened May 10, 1907
Babb, Cook & Willard, Architects

Fort Washington Branch Library
535-7 West 179th Street
Opened March 14, 1914
Cook & Welch, Architects

Continued

* *Decommissioned*
** *Decommissoned and No Longer Standing*

Hamilton Grange Branch Library
503 West 145th Street
Opened January 8, 1907
McKim, Mead & White, Architects

Hamilton Fish Park Branch**
388-92 East Houston Street
Opened September 12, 1909
Carrere & Hastings, Architects

Harlem Branch Library
9-11 West 124th Street
Opened January 11, 1909
McKim, Mead & White, Architects

Hudson Park Branch Library
66 Leroy Street
Opened January 24, 1906
Carrere & Hastings, Architects

Muhlenberg Branch Library
209-11 West 23rd Street
Opened February 19, 1906
Carrere & Hastings, Architects

96th Street Branch Regional Library
112-4 East 96th Street
Opened September 22, 1905
Babb, Cook & Willard, Architects

115th Street Branch Library
203 West 115th Street
Opened November 6, 1908
McKim, Mead & White, Architects

125th Street Branch Library
224 East 125th Street
Opened March 7, 1904
McKim, Mead & White, Architects

Riverside Branch**
190-2 Amsterdam Avenue
Opened February 16, 1905
Carrere & Hastings, Architects

Rivington Branch*
61-3 Rivington Street
Opened June 10, 1905
McKim, Mead & White, Architects

St. Agnes Branch Library
444-6 Amsterdam Avenue
Opened March 26, 1906
Babb, Cook & Willard, Architects

St. Gabriel's Park Branch**
303-5 East 36th Street
Opened May 15, 1908
McKim, Mead & White, Architects

Schomburg Collection for Research
in Black Culture
103 West 135th Street
Opened July 14, 1905
McKim, Mead & White, Architects

Seward Park Branch Library
192 East Broadway
Opened November 11, 1909
Babb, Cook & Welch, Architects

67th Street Branch Library
328 East 67th Street
Opened January 20, 1905
Babb, Cook & Willard, Architects

Tompkins Square Branch Library
331 East 10th Street
Opened December 1, 1904
McKim, Mead & White, Architects

Washington Heights Branch Library
1000-02 St. Nicholas Avenue
Opened February 26, 1914
Carrere & Hastings, Architects

Webster Branch Library
1465 York Avenue
Opened October 24, 1906
Babb, Cook & Willard, Architects

West 40th Street Branch*
457 West 40th Street
Opened October 20, 1913
Cook & Welch, Architects

Yorkville Branch Library
222 East 79th Street
Opened December 13, 1902
James Brown Lord, Architect

Continued

* *Decommissioned*
** *Decommissoned and No Longer Standing*

THE NEW YORK PUBLIC LIBRARY
STATEN ISLAND

Port Richmond Branch Library
75 Bennett Street
Opened March 18, 1905
Carrere & Hastings, Architects

St. George Branch Borough Library Center
10 Central Avenue/450 St. Mark's Place
Opened June 26, 1907
Carrere & Hastings, Architects

Stapleton Branch Library
132 Canal Street
Opened June 17, 1907
Carrere & Hastings, Architects

Tottenville Branch Library
7430 Amboy Road
Opened November 26, 1904
Carrere & Hastings, Architects

THE QUEENS BOROUGH PUBLIC
LIBRARY

Astoria Branch Library
14-01 Astoria Boulevard
Opened November 19, 1904
Tuthill & Higgins, Architects

Elmhurst Branch Library
86-01 Broadway
Opened March 31, 1906
Lord & Hewlett, Architects

Far Rockaway Branch**
1637 Central Avenue
Opened August 18, 1904
Lord & Hewlett, Architects

Flushing Branch**
41-25 Main Street
Opened December 17, 1906
Lord & Hewlett, Architects

Poppenhusen Branch Library
121-23 14th Avenue
Opened October 5, 1904
Heins & LaFarge, Architects

Richmond Hill Branch Library
118-14 Hillside Avenue
Opened July 1, 1905
Tuthill & Higgins, Architects

Woodhaven Branch Library
85-41 Forest Parkway
Opened January 5, 1924
Robert F. Schirmer, Architect

*   *Decommissioned*
** *Decommissoned and No Longer Standing*

INVENTORY OF CARNEGIE LIBRARIES OF NEW YORK CITY

BROOKLYN PUBLIC LIBRARY

BROOKLYN

☆ ●Greenpoint

★ *Leonard*

★ *Bushwick*

Williamsburgh ★

●Brooklyn Heights
Business Library

★ *Washington
Irving*

★ ●Marcy

Walt Whitman ★ *DeKalb*

●Clinton Hill

★ *Macon*

★ *Carroll Gardens*

★ *Saratoga*

★ *Arlington*

Pacific ★

★ *Bedford*

●Brower Park

☆ ●Red Hook

●Central Library

Cypress
Hills

★ *Brownsville*

★ *Park Slope*

★ *Eastern Parkway*

●New Lots

★ *Stone Avenue*

●Spring Creek

●Crown Heights

●East Flatbush

Sunset Park

Flatbush ★

●Rugby

☆

●Windsor Terrace

●Carnarsie

South Branch

●Borough Park

●Cortelyou

●Clarendon

Jamaica Bay ●

●Bay Ridge

●Kensington

Paerdegat ●

McKinley Park

●Mapleton

●Midwood

●Flatlands

★

●Dyker

●Ryder

●Mill Basin

Ft. Hamilton

New Utrecht ●

●Highlawn

●Kings Highway

●Homecrest

●Kings Bay

Gerritsen Beach ●

●Gravesend

●Sheepshead Bay

Ulmer Park

●Brighton Beach

●Coney Island

Brooklyn
Public Library 1996

★ *Operating Carnegie Libraries*

☆ *Former Carnegie Libraries or sites*

Arlington Branch Library, Exterior, 1994, Lisa Clifford, DGS Photographer; Interior, n.d., c. 1906, F.A. Walter Photographer, (Brooklyn Public Library – Brooklyn Collection)

ARLINGTON BRANCH

Address   203 ARLINGTON AVENUE
Borough   BROOKLYN
Date   1906
Architects RICHARD A. WALKER/WALKER & MORRIS

Description: The Arlington Branch is located in a quiet residential neighborhood of two and three story houses dating from the late 19th and early 20th centuries. The library blends in with the architecture of the area, although it is more formal than the masonry and frame residences. The library is located on a large corner site running along Arlington and through to both Warwick and Ashford Streets. A lawn surrounds the building, enclosed by the original delicate wrought iron fence. A similar fence has been added to the entrance steps. Small shrubs, apparently not part of the original design, judging from early photographs, have been planted in the front. There are also mature trees on the property. The landscaping was not done immediately after the building was built. In 1908 the *Brooklyn Eagle* (8/1/1908) reported that residents in fashionable Arlington complained about the apology for a lawn around the library.

The graceful two story Classical Revival style red brick building has stone trim and an asphalt roof. The recessed central entrance of the five bay structure is marked by a triangular pediment. Brick pilasters separate the bays. A flag originally hung from a pole extending from the entrance pediment. The builder was L. W. Seaman Company, with offices at 187 Grand Avenue in Brooklyn. The *New York World* (11/11/1906) declared that the library was the largest and finest of its kind. Although handsome with excellent proportions, it was actually one of the smaller Carnegie branches in Brooklyn. The spectacular 7,000 square foot interior is almost entirely intact and remains one of the best preserved Carnegies in New York City. The large, two-story central delivery room is flanked by graceful wooden stairs leading to the reading rooms. The natural oak trim is intact, as are the paneled columns and decorative railing at the mezzanine. The skylight has been filled in but the framing is visible from the reading rooms and from the attic. There are wood paneled reading nooks with charming mantels in the two reading rooms, one originally for children and one for adults. The lower level contains workrooms and meeting rooms.

Alterations include replacement of the windows and entrance door. Metal security grates have been added to the windows and suspended fluorescent lighting has been installed.   There was a major rehabilitation in 1951-2, a period when several Brooklyn branch libraries were renovated.   There was another major rehabilitation in 1980.

Notes: The library was originally known as the East Branch and this name is still on the cornice frieze. It was officially opened on November 7, 1906. *The Brooklyn Standard* (11/11/1906) reported a large attendance at the opening. David Boody, President of the Carnegie Committee, presented the building to the City. Robert W. Hubbard, Commissioner of Charities accepted for the City. *NY Herald* (11/11/1906) The cost of the site was $19,340 and the building and equipment $80,826, for a total of $100,166.

Current Information: This is the Arlington Branch of the Brooklyn Public Library. There are plans to make the library accessible to the disabled.

Bedford Branch Library, Exterior, 1994, Lisa Clifford, DGS Photographer; Interior, n.d.,
c.1906, F.A. Walter Photographer, Brooklyn Public Library – Brooklyn Collection

BEDFORD BRANCH

Address   496 FRANKLIN AVENUE
Borough   BROOKLYN
Date   1905
Architects LORD & HEWLETT

Description: The library is located on a busy commercial street in a residential neighborhood. The neighborhood is composed of two to four story 19th century masonry row houses and other 19th and early 20th century masonry structures. There is a school nearby and a vacant lot next door. The library is a freestanding structure located in the middle of the blockfront and surrounded by a small plot of ground. There is a lawn in front and a concrete parking lot on the sides where there was once a sunken garden leading to the basement entrance.   The property is enclosed by an original simple wrought iron fence, with a similar fence added to the front entrance.

The handsome two story Classical revival style structure is brick with prominent stone trim. The three bay library has a central entrance reached by a flight of steps. The entrance door and the two flanking windows have monumental stone surrounds with foliate carving, topped by a dentillated cornice and asphalt roof. Robert J. Mahoney, General Contractor, was the builder. The Brooklyn Public Library wanted to buy an adjacent lot for the auditorium, but the Board of Estimate turned down the request *Brooklyn Times* (4/24 & 1/17/1903). The 15,000 plus square foot interior plan is largely intact, with the delivery desk in the center and reading rooms on the sides on the first floor.   The reading rooms have their original stone mantels. The stacks are still at the rear behind the delivery desk. The second floor was used for class rooms and is now a learning center. The original architects selected the Clark & Baker furniture and stacks and Black & Boyd light fixtures, all of which have since been removed from the library.

Alterations include replacement of the windows and entrance door and the filling in of the door transom. The lamp posts at the entrance have been removed and an awning has been added to the rear wing. Interior changes include new partitions, a later vestibule, modern fluorescent lighting and vinyl flooring. The heating, ventilation and air conditioning systems were upgraded in 1982.

Notes: The library officially opened on February 4, 1905 with addresses by Reverend Dr. Cadman and Edward P. Lyon. The cost of the site was $24,000, the cost of the building and equipment $90,962 for a total of $114,962. The Bedford Branch of the Brooklyn Public Library was previously located on the ground floor of Avon Hall before the Carnegie library was built. The Bedford and Williamsburgh Branches were featured in the March, 1903 *Library Journal* article on the planning of the Brooklyn Public Library branches and were considered excellent examples of planning and design. Bedford was one of the first five Carnegie libraries built in Brooklyn, along with DeKalb, Greenpoint (demolished), Pacific, and Williamsburgh. The plans and elevations for all five, each by a different architect, were extensively publicized and were praised for their thoughtful plans and attention to light, air, and accommodation of people and books.

Current Information: This is the Bedford Branch of the Brooklyn Public Library. Improvements are planned to stabilize and improve the side and rear yards, and to make the branch accessible.

Brownsville Branch Library, Exterior, 1994, Lisa Clifford, DGS Photographer; Interior, n.d., c. 1908, The Walter Studio, (Brooklyn Public Library – Brooklyn Collection)

BROWNSVILLE BRANCH

Address   61 GLENMORE AVENUE
Borough   BROOKLYN
Date   1908
Architects LORD & HEWLETT

Description: The library, once bound by one to four story wood and masonry residences, is now surrounded by high-rise public housing structures. An original street tree remains in front of the library. The branch is surrounded by a simple, later, wrought iron fence. It is similar to the original wrought iron fence, but several feet higher. The freestanding building has a small lawn around it.

The simple two story, five bay brick library is topped by a dentillated cornice. There is a projecting center entrance with Ionic columns flanking the door. The sash in the main windows have been replaced and metal grates have been added. The unusual small windows below the main ones have been tiled in. On the inside, the book shelves flanked these windows. The entrance steps and door have been altered. The builder was John T. Brady & Company, with offices at 103 Park Avenue. This company also built the Fort Hamilton Carnegie Library, also for Lord & Hewlett and the Red Hook Carnegie Library, for the architect Richard A. Walker. Like the exterior, the 10,000 plus square foot interior was also simple in design, with prominent hanging light fixtures supplied by Black & Boyd. They have been replaced with fluorescent light fixtures. In 1939, Leonard Jenkins was commissioned to paint a monumental mural on the inside "The History of Ships," but it has apparently been removed or painted over. The two mantels in the reading rooms have survived intact.

The windows have been replaced and metal security grates have been added. A fire in 1922, a rehabilitation in 1960-63 and a major rehabilitation including roof repair in 1986-9 brought changes to the building. It was closed for the repairs twice, in the 1960's and 1980's.

Notes: The library was officially opened on December 19, 1908 with addresses by Dr. Martin A. Meyer, Simon F. Rothschild and Reverend S.I. Finklestein. David Boody, President of the Carnegie Committee, presented the library to Herman A. Metz, Comptroller, representing New York City and to Edward Kaufmann, representing the Brooklyn Public Library. Muller's orchestra provided the music, for this opening and nearly all of the others. Fifteen thousand people attended the ceremony *New York Times*, 12/20/1908. The neighborhood was growing so drastically that the building was enlarged before it was finished. In addition, the Brownsville Children's Library, now the Stone Avenue Branch, was built in 1914 to relieve the crowding. The site cost $24,000 and the building and equipment $90,962, for a total cost of $114,962. When the site was being selected there were letters to the Carnegie Committee recommending several sites in the neighborhood, but the final site chosen was the one recommended by the site agent for the Carnegie Committee, Alanson T. Briggs. This was characteristic of the site-selection process for the Carnegies, which were very much in demand in the neighborhoods.

Current Information: This is the Brownsville Branch of the Brooklyn Public Library. Current projects aim to make the building accessible to all patrons and also call for waterproofing the facade.

Bushwick Branch Library, Exterior, 1994, Lisa Clifford, DGS Photographer; Interior, 1909, F.A. Walter Photographer, (Brooklyn Public Library – Brooklyn Collection)

BUSHWICK BRANCH

Address   340 BUSHWICK AVENUE
Borough   BROOKLYN
Date   1908
Architect RAYMOND F. ALMIRALL

Description: Once surrounded by low rise wood and masonry residences, the library is now in the midst of mid-and-high rise public housing. It is across the street from a school. The library is located on a corner site and was originally built close to the property line, with a small lawn in front. Now the original lawn has been replaced and there is a wide sidewalk in front. The building is surrounded by a simple wrought iron fence similar to the original, but several feet higher. The fence now extends to enclose the entrance steps.

The two story Classical Revival style red brick building has fluted columns with foliate carving. The five bay building has a slightly projecting entrance bay with an elaborate arched pediment above the door. The builder was John W. Schaefer, Jr. & Company. The 10,000 plus square foot interior had high ceilings with pendant light fixtures supplied by Sterling Bronze Company. The contractor appears to have selected the furnishings. There are lowered ceilings and later fluorescent lights on the inside today.

Alterations include replacement of the windows and the entrance door, which also has a filled-in transom. Metal security grates have been added to the windows. There is a recent second story rear addition. The library was closed for renovation in 1957, for repairs to damage caused, in part, by crime and vandalism. Changes on the interior include suspended ceilings and fluorescent lighting.

Notes: The library opened officially on December 16, 1908 with addresses by Leon Louria, MD and the Honorable Mitchell May. David Boody, President of the Carnegie Committee, presented the library to Patrick F. McGowan, President of the Board of Aldermen, representing New York City and to James McKeen, representing the Brooklyn Public Library. Before the Carnegie library was built the Bushwick branch of the Brooklyn Public Library was housed on the ground floor of a church. It burned in 1903 *Brooklyn Eagle* February, 1903. Muller's orchestra provided the music for the opening, and most of the other Carnegies. The cost of the site was $53,802. The cost of the building was $58,473, for a total of $112,275. (Reported in the 1914 *Record of Real Estate Owned by the City of New York.*)

Current Information: This is the Bushwick Branch of the Brooklyn Public Library. The current renovation projects underway include conformance with the Americans with Disabilities Act as well as heating, ventilation, and electrical improvements.

Carroll Gardens Branch Library, Exterior, 1994, Lisa Clifford, DGS Photographer; Interior, n.d., c.1905–1915, F.A. Walter Photographer, (Brooklyn Public Library – Brooklyn Collection)

CARROLL GARDENS BRANCH

Address   396 CLINTON STREET
Borough   BROOKLYN
Date   1905
Architect   WILLIAM B. TUBBY

Description: The library is located in a quiet residential neighborhood of 19th century, masonry, three and four story row houses and small early 20th century apartment buildings. The building sits on a corner site and is built to the building line in front. There is a simple wrought iron fence surrounding the site with new iron fencing added at the entrance.

The tall, one story Classical Revival style building has a recessed central entrance marked by two, full-height brick Ionic columns. The arched entrance and the windows soar to the full height of the building. A pediment topped by a balustrade crowns the facade. In a report on the opening, the building was called "a model one in every respect, large, airy, well lighted, and perfectly equipped." (*BPL Clipping File,* "Carroll Gardens Branch," 1905, no attribution). The builder was John Thatcher & Son, who also built the Flatbush Carnegie Branch for R. L. Daus, Architect.

The large, 14,000 plus square foot interior has the original dramatic barrel-vaulted ceiling supported by columns. The stacks are at the rear with an altered balcony. There is an original mantel with decorative plaques in the reading room, and an early or original wood paneled screen.

There is a modern aluminum projecting curved doorway, modern aluminum windows, and metal mesh security grilles at the first floor windows. The vestibule plan has been altered, the skylight filled in, and modern rectangular light fixtures have been installed. The building had major renovations, including a new roof, in 1950-51. Janitor's quarters were installed in the basement in the 1950 renovation but do not exist today.

Notes: The library was originally called the Carroll Park Branch. The name was changed to the Carroll Gardens Branch in 1973.   The library officially opened on March 3, 1905. David Boody, President of the Carnegie Committee, presented the library to Alfred J. Talley, Civil Service Commissioner representing New York City, in front of a crowd of 700. There were addresses by Reverend Dr. Albert J. Lyman and James F. McGee, President of the Board of Trade. The fifth Carnegie library erected in Brooklyn, it opened with a staff of six librarians.   The cost of the site was $25,000, the building and equipment $81,293 with a total cost of $106, 293.

Current Information: This is the Carroll Gardens Branch of the Brooklyn Public Library. The current project calls for the design and construction of a new fence and auditorium steps.

DeKalb Branch Library, Exterior, 1994, Lisa Clifford, DGS Photographer; Interior, n.d., c. 1905, F.A. Walter Photographer, (Brooklyn Public Library – Brooklyn Collection)

DEKALB BRANCH

Address   784 BUSHWICK AVENUE
Borough   BROOKLYN
Date   1905
Architect   WILLIAM B. TUBBY

Description: The library is located on a busy, wide street in a mostly residential neighborhood, with some commercial buildings. The surrounding architecture dates from the last half of the 19th century to the early 20th century and consists primarily of two and three story masonry row houses and four story brick tenements. There are two school buildings across the street from the library. The library is on a corner site, on a small terrace, enclosed by a wrought iron fence. There are three different types of fence, dating from different periods. The ornate DeKalb Street fence sits atop a brick wall.

The exuberant two story, three bay Classical Revival style brick library has a hipped standing seam metal roof ending in a brick balustrade with stone balusters. The two-story high center entrance and the flanking windows are surrounded by elaborate rusticated stone trim. An early elevation for the library showed more stone trim, probably reduced for budgetary concerns. The 12,000 plus square foot interior had a skylit center delivery room with two-tiered stacks at the rear which still remain with their original decorative railing. The skylight has been roofed over. As in the original plan, reading rooms are located on either side of the delivery room. There was a large lecture hall in the basement. The *Brooklyn Citizen* (1/27/1903) stated that a great deal of attention was given to the question of lighting, citing the large, two story windows.

The builder was F. J. Kelly's Sons, a Brooklyn firm with offices on Dean Street. There was a delay in finishing construction and the company was reported to have been troubled by strikes. The builder was also responsible for the Leonard and Stone Avenue Carnegie Libraries, both also designed by Tubby.

The entrance door has been altered but the windows are original or have their original fenestration pattern. A metal sign was placed above the door in about 1935 and the cartouche was removed. The library was rehabilitated in 1950-1, when the present fluorescent lighting was installed along with plumbing, heating and electrical renovations and general construction. Additional construction took place in 1969 to repair damage due to vandalism.

Notes: The library was officially opened on February 11, 1905. The site cost $28,000, the building and equipment $92,937 for a total cost of $120,937. The library was featured in *A Portfolio of Carnegie Libraries* in 1907. This was one of the first five Carnegie libraries built in Brooklyn. The other four were Bedford, Greenpoint (demolished), Pacific, and Williamsburgh. The plans and elevations for all five, each by a different architect, were extensively publicized. They received praise for their thoughtfulness and attention to such practical matters as light, air, and accommodation of people and books.

Current Information: This is the DeKalb Branch of the Brooklyn Public Library. The building is slated for modifications to make it accessible to the handicapped to be designed by Allanbrook Benic Czajka Architects.

Eastern Parkway Branch Library, Exterior, 1994, Lisa Clifford, DGS Photographer;
Rendering by Raymond Almirall, c. 1914, (Brooklyn Public Library – Brooklyn Collection)

EASTERN PARKWAY BRANCH

Address	1044 EASTERN PARKWAY
Borough	BROOKLYN
Date	1914
Architect	RAYMOND F. ALMIRALL

Description: The library is located in a residential neighborhood and is surrounded by early 20th century two to four story apartment buildings. It is situated on Eastern Parkway, the designated New York City Scenic landmark designed as the first parkway in the United States by Frederick Law Olmsted and Calvert Vaux in 1870-74. The library is on a corner site, built to the building line on the sides and set back in front. A simple, apparently original iron fence encloses the front yard; a later fence has been added to the entrance.

The one story, five bay library has a center entrance reached by a flight of steps, a characteristic Carnegie library feature. There is a stone balustrade at the flat roof. The large arched windows dominate the stone facade. The builder was Luke A. Burke & Sons. The over 12,000 square foot interior had high ceilings, now dropped, and hanging light fixtures, now modern fluorescent. Frank Hill, Head Librarian when the Brooklyn Carnegies were planned and built, was actively involved in the planning, giving comments on the proposed plans. There is an original reading nook with a mantel with decorative tile, wood paneling, and an uncharacteristically decorative plaster ceiling.

The entrance door has been replaced, the windows are early or original, with the original fenestration pattern. The vestibule has been altered and a dropped ceiling has been added. New partitions have been added to the first floor. The building was rehabilitated in 1950-51, had heating, ventilation, air conditioning and mechanical system upgrades in 1969 and received another general rehabilitation in 1975.

Notes: The library was officially opened on July 7, 1914 to the sounds of Muller Music, the traditional orchestra. The site cost $21,500 and the cost of the building and equipment, as reported by the Brooklyn Public Library, was $108,439.

Current Information: This is the Eastern Parkway Branch of the Brooklyn Public Library. Current renovation projects will improve accessibility and will focus on air conditioning enhancement.

Flatbush Branch Library, Exterior, 1994, Lisa Clifford, DGS Photographer; Interior, n.d., c. 1910– 1915, N. L. Stebbins Photographer, (Brooklyn Public Library – Brooklyn Collection)

FLATBUSH BRANCH

Address   22 LINDEN BOULEVARD
Borough   BROOKLYN
Date   1905
Architect   R. L. DAUS

Description: The library is located in the middle of the block front with a small lawn in front. The building is located one building east of busy commercial Flatbush Avenue on a residential block of three to six story apartment buildings primarily dating from the early 20th century.

This library has had several major alterations. Originally, it was a two story, three bay brick building with modest stone trim. The projecting center entrance had brick columns with cartouches and a door with a triangular pediment.   A molded stone cornice topped the library. The original interior had a central delivery room flanked by reading rooms, with two-tiered stacks in the rear, behind Corinthian columns. There were pilasters, columns, arched openings, and hanging bronze light fixtures.

The building was enlarged to over 22,000 square feet and completely redesigned in 1937 by Brooklyn Public Works with WPA funds. John R. Petter was the supervising architect, Jack C. Street the designer and delineator. The front was altered, with a new elevation including WPA Moderne window spandrels, and an altered one story entrance bay. Two, one story wings at the east and west ends were built. There are intact elements from 1905, including the round plaster columns and the balcony above the stacks on the first floor, the wooden stairs with turned balusters, and oak sliding doors, woodwork and stacks on the second floor. The 1930's Moderne vestibule, with its marble paneling and nickel steel railing, is intact. There was another major renovation in 1953, with the basement being finished for an auditorium as well as repair and redecoration. There was a fire in 1957 requiring repairs and another rehabilitation in 1966-9. In 1978 the roof was upgraded and electrical work was done.

Notes: The library was officially opened on October 7, 1905. The site cost $16,000, the building and equipment cost $70,315, totaling $86,316. There were heated discussions over the location of the library and whether it should be located east or west of Flatbush Avenue. Ultimately it was placed east of the avenue.

Current Information: This is the Flatbush Branch of the Brooklyn Public Library. The library is slated for major rehabilitation, including extensive exterior and interior renovations and Americans with Disabilities Act improvements, to be designed by Margaret Helfand Architects.

Ft. Hamilton Branch Library, Exterior, 1994, Lisa Clifford, DGS Photographer; Interior, n.d.,
c. 1910– 1915, F.A. Walter Photographer, (Brooklyn Public Library – Brooklyn Collection)

FORT HAMILTON BRANCH

Address   FOURTH AVENUE & 95TH STREET
Borough   BROOKLYN
Date   1907
Architects   LORD & HEWLETT

Description: The library is situated on a busy two-way commercial street lined primarily with three story masonry commercial buildings. It is located on a corner site surrounded by lawn. The banks of shrubs around the building are an original landscape feature. There is a simple, later iron fence surrounding the site and modern fencing at the entrance.

This simple five bay, two story, brick Classical Revival style library has a hipped roof. The center entrance is marked by limestone trim and a modest pediment. The windows are placed high on the facade, below the overhanging eaves of the hipped roof. The builder was John T. Brady & Company, who also built the Brownsville Carnegie for Lord & Hewlett, the Red Hook Branch for Walker & Morris, and the Hamilton Fish Park, Hudson Park and High Bridge Carnegie Branches for Carrere & Hastings, Architects.

The interior has been renovated and currently has a dropped ceiling and modern fluorescent light fixtures. The bronze chandelier over the delivery desk was removed but the rectangular plaster columns have survived. One of the two original tiled fireplaces with wood paneled surrounds remains.

The chimney was raised in 1912 because of an imperfect draught. In this year, a lawn and fence were installed. Today, the entrance door has been made smaller, small side windows were bricked in, and the door and windows have been replaced. The cornice modillions were removed and replaced by a later frieze, and the original skylight was roofed over. The mechanical, heating, ventilation and air conditioning systems were upgraded in 1975.

Notes: The library was officially opened on October 7, 1905. The Fifth Artillery Band played at the ceremony; David A. Boody, President of the Carnegie Committee, and John Hill Morgan of the Brooklyn Public Library gave addresses. There had been a Fort Hamilton Free Library in the community before its services were assumed by the new branch library. The Carnegie site cost $13,567; the building $31,970; the total cost was $45,537.

Current Information: This is the Fort Hamilton Branch of the Brooklyn Public Library. The library is slated for renovations to make it accessible to the handicapped.

Greenpoint Branch Library, Exterior, n.d., c. 1906, F.A. Walter Photographer; Interior, n.d., c. 1906, (Brooklyn Public Library – Brooklyn Collection)

GREENPOINT BRANCH

Address	107 NORMAN AVENUE
Borough	BROOKLYN
Date	1906
Architect	R. L. DAUS

Description: The Carnegie library was located on a corner lot, but the building took up most of the site. In his speech at the opening George H. Rowe, editor of the *Greenpoint Star*, described the importance of the library to the community. "For years Greenpoint has been derisively referred to on the vaudeville stage and the criticism in many instances came from those who had no conception of home and who generally carried their earthly possessions on their backs. We needed just such a place as this, where the general public could turn on the faucets and drink deep from the fountains of intellectuality" *Greenpoint Star* 4/14/1906.

The elaborate three bay, two story Classical Revival brick building had stone trim and a stone balustrade at the roof. The projecting center entrance had a high flight of steps leading up to a door with a triangular pediment. The architect was dissatisfied with the quality of the work of the contractor, P. J. Carlin & Company, complaining of the buckling sheet iron cornice and flooding due to inadequate damp proofing. These problems were remedied and the *Greenpoint Star* (April 14, 1906) called it a "Handsome new building [which] pleased all who had the opportunity to inspect it." The nearly 16,000 square foot interior had the characteristic plan of center delivery desk flanked by reading rooms. It was praised for its tasteful simplicity by the *Greenpoint Star* (4/7/1906). According to the paper the woodwork was golden oak and the brasswork had a dull rather than shiny finish. The stacks at the rear were separated by Composite columns. The interior was similar to the architect's Flatbush Branch, since altered.

In 1944 the library closed, due to a manpower shortage but by 1951 the Greenpoint librarians received the Friends of the Brooklyn Public Library Award. That same year the building was declared to be in wretched condition. It was demolished in 1970 for a new library.

Notes: The Carnegie library was officially opened on April 7, 1906. Borough President Coler gave an address in the crowded auditorium. Daniel W. McWilliams, Vice-President of the Carnegie Committee presented the library to Brooklyn Borough President Coler, representing New York City. Muller's orchestra provided the music, for this opening and nearly all of the rest. The site, which consisted of eight separately owned lots, cost $39,922; the building cost $95,877 and the total cost was $135,800. This was one of the first five Carnegie libraries built in Brooklyn, along with Bedford, DeKalb, Pacific, and Williamsburgh. The plans and elevations for all five, each by a different architect, were extensively publicized and were praised for their thoughtful plans and attention to such practical matters as light, air, and accommodation of people and books.

Current Information: The current library was opened in 1973 on the site of the original Carnegie library. The new building is the home of the Greenpoint Branch of the Brooklyn Public Library.

Leonard Branch Library, Exterior, 1994, Lisa Clifford, DGS Photographer;
Interior, n.d., c. 1908, (Brooklyn Public Library – Brooklyn Collection)

LEONARD BRANCH

Address	81 DEVOE STREET
Borough	BROOKLYN
Date	1908
Architect	WILLIAM B. TUBBY

Description: The library is located in a residential community filled with three and four story frame and masonry houses built during the later 19th and early 20th centuries. It is one block from commercial Metropolitan Avenue. The library is located on a corner lot and had originally a small lawn around it. The site is enclosed by a simple iron fence, similar to but taller than the original.

The one story, five bay brick building has a projecting center entrance and a slate roof. The doorway is trimmed in stone, with a bracketed pediment above. The austere classical library has rectangular windows set high on the facade, similar to the Fort Hamilton Carnegie library, designed by Lord & Hewlett. The builder was the firm of F. J. Kelly's Sons who were responsible for two other William Tubby-designed Carnegie Libraries, DeKalb and Stone Avenue. The 10,000 plus square foot interior is simple in design. There were wood trimmed windows, wood paneling, and a molded plaster ceiling with skylights. There is now a lowered ceiling and the wood paneling is no longer visible.

The entrance door and the windows have been replaced and the front entrance steps have been altered. On the inside, the ceiling has been lowered, fluorescent lights have replaced the original pendant fixtures and a new vestibule has been added. There was a major rehabilitation in the 1950's, with a new roof and interior trim. The library was rehabilitated in 1966-9 and again 1978.

Notes: The library was officially opened on December 1, 1908. David A. Boody, President of the Carnegie Committee, presented the library to Patrick F. McGowan, President of the Board of Alderman, representing New York City and John Hill Morgan, representing the Brooklyn Public Library. There were addresses by Honorable George W. Schaedle, Reverend Edward J. McGoldrick and Dr. P. Virdone. The site cost $27,500; the building and equipment cost $56,765; the total cost was $84,265. The Board of Estimate appropriated $10,000 for books in 1906.

Current Information: This is the Leonard Branch of the Brooklyn Public Library. The roof was replaced on this building in 1980.

Macon Branch Library, Exterior, 1994, Lisa Clifford, DGS Photographer; Interior, n.d., c. 1907, F.A. Walter Photographer, Brooklyn Public Library – Brooklyn Collection

MACON BRANCH

Address   361 LEWIS AVENUE
Borough   BROOKLYN
Date   1907
Architects RICHARD A. WALKER/WALKER & MORRIS

Description: The library is located in a residential neighborhood of three to four story 19th century masonry row houses. Lewis Avenue is a commercial and residential street with 20th century masonry buildings. Located on a corner site, the building takes up most of the lot. The library sits on a platform which rises one step up from the sidewalk. A simple, later iron fence encloses the site and the front door.

The two story, five bay Classical Revival style red brick library has Indiana limestone trim around the door and windows. The center entrance is set apart by a stone surround topped by a cartouche. The windows are located high on the facade, just under the dentillated classical cornice. Two pillars at the front entrance once held lamps. The builder was Daniel Ryan, who had offices at 723 Third Avenue in Manhattan. The interior has large reading rooms and smaller alcoves containing original fireplaces and wooden benches. There were large frescoes above the mantels and decorative panels with axioms such as "No Gain Without Pain" on either side. The frescoes are no longer visible. The original delivery desk is characteristically in the center and the stacks, with their original mezzanine metal railing, are at the rear. There is original oak paneling on the walls and original bookshelves. The *Brooklyn Eagle* called it one of the best lighted of all of the branches (7/16/1907).

The entrance door and the windows have been replaced. The current asphalt roof is probably a later cladding. There was a major rehabilitation in 1948-9. In 1973-7 the interior was modernized, a new auditorium was built, new fluorescent lighting was installed and the mechanical systems - heating, ventilation and air conditioning - were upgraded.

Notes: The library officially opened on July 15, 1907. It was the eleventh opening and 2000 people attended. *Brooklyn Citizen* (7/16/1907) David A. Boody, President of the Carnegie Committee, presented the library to Bird S. Coler, Brooklyn Borough President, representing New York City and Edward Kaufmann, representing the Brooklyn Public Library. There were addresses by Reverend Robert J. Kent and Robert H. Roy. The site cost $22,000; the building and equipment cost $71,481 for a total of $93,481. The Board of Estimate appropriated $10,000 for books in 1906.

Current Information: This is the Macon Branch of the Brooklyn Public Library. Current projects include an upgrade of the air conditioning systems, improvements to make the building accessible to all patrons, and installation of a new roof which will replicate the appearance of the original slate roof. The roof project is being designed by Leslie Feder Architect.

Pacific Branch Library, Exterior, 1994, Lisa Clifford, DGS Photographer; Interior, n.d., c. 1903, Frank Pearsall Photographer, (Brooklyn Public Library – Brooklyn Collection)

PACIFIC BRANCH

Address   25 FOURTH AVENUE
Borough   BROOKLYN
Date   1903
Architect RAYMOND F. ALMIRALL

Description: The Pacific Branch is located on a busy two-way street in a neighborhood that was originally made up of low rise wood and masonry residences. Today the area is a mix of industrial, commercial and residential buildings, with one to six story structures dating from the nineteenth through the twentieth centuries. The library is located on a corner site, occupying most of the lot. A later fence borders the property and later steps and rails lead to the front door.

The two story, three bay Classical Revival style brick building has an unusual hipped and conical roof topped by a dormer at the ridgeline. The first floor center doorway and flanking windows have Tudor style arches with keystone surrounds as well as the old Brooklyn Public Library emblem above the door. The architect, Raymond Almirall, described his sketches of the library as being modeled after the idea of the New Jersey Historical Society. The builder was Church Construction Company, which also built the Park Slope Carnegie branch for Raymond Almirall.

The 15,000 plus square foot interior has a semi-circular plan with two-story stacks in that configuration at the rear, a plan also used for the Williamsburgh Carnegie Library. The plan type was admired by *The Library Journal* in a March, 1903 article for being full of light and well coordinated for effective and economical administration. The series of 1939 WPA murals on the wall over the built-in bookcases are no longer extant. Wood paneled stairs lead to the spectacular second floor reading room, with its dramatic tiled fireplace with a carved wooden screen and wood paneling on the walls.

Raymond Almirall was hired as the architect in charge of the restoration when the building was damaged by subway construction in 1914 and by fire in 1917. The upper part of the cornice was simplified in 1951. The community saved the library from demolition after a fire in 1973 and it was rehabilitated in 1975. The windows, entrance steps and door, and the lanterns at the door are later, although not modern, replacements.

Notes: The library officially opened on October 8, 1903. The site cost $29,000; the building $98,683, with a total $127, 683. This was one of the first five Carnegie libraries built in Brooklyn along with Bedford, DeKalb, Greenpoint (demolished), and Williamsburgh.   The plans and elevations for all five, each by a different architect, were extensively publicized and were praised for their thoughtful plans and attention to such practical matters as light, air, and accommodation of people and books. The Pacific Branch Library was the first Carnegie opened in Brooklyn.

Current Information: This is the Pacific Branch of the Brooklyn Public Library.

Park Slope Branch Library, Exterior, 1994, Lisa Clifford, DGS Photographer;
Interior, n.d., c. 1906, (Brooklyn Public Library – Brooklyn Collection)

PARK SLOPE BRANCH

Address   431 SIXTH AVENUE
Borough   BROOKLYN
Date   1906
Architect RAYMOND F. ALMIRALL

Description: The library is located in a residential neighborhood of 19th and early 20th century row houses and small apartment buildings, adjacent to the Park Slope Historic District. It is across the street from the 1876-7 P.S. 39, a designated New York City landmark and one block from a YMCA. The old branch library was located across the street from the new Carnegie. There is a lawn with a later iron fence around the property.

The large two story, seven bay Classical Revival style building has a monumental projecting center entrance with four Doric columns supporting a stone pediment. The gable-ended sides of the brick building are faced in limestone, with a formal classical pediment supported by double pilasters at the corners. The *Brooklyn Citizen* called this branch imposing and the most pretentious of the many Carnegies (July, 1906). The builder, the Church Construction Company, was also responsible for Raymond Almirall's Pacific Carnegie Branch and the South Branch Carnegie, designed by Lord & Hewlett.

The spectacular, largely intact interior has stained glass arched entrances supported by freestanding columns leading from the delivery room to the reading rooms and stacks. The uncharacteristically ornate interior also has pedimented window trim, two tiled fireplaces, and wood paneling stretching nearly to the ceiling and a vestibule with a vaulted stained glass ceiling, marble mosaic flooring and two entrances on either side leading to the main reading room. The Head Librarian Frank Hill did not consider its plan efficient and stated that it interfered with good circulation, but time has apparently proven him wrong.

The exterior steps and entrance door have been replaced; the windows have the same fenestration pattern as the originals. On the interior, the original pendant light fixtures were replaced, as was the original cork carpet and original bookcases. The library underwent a major rehabilitation in 1948-9.

Notes: The library was officially opened as the Prospect Branch on July 30, 1906. The name was changed to the Park Slope Branch in 1975. David A. Boody, President of the Carnegie Committee, presided over the ceremonies. This branch replaced one of the first libraries in the area, the Litchfield Mansion library. (*Brooklyn Eagle*, July, 1906) The site cost $35,000; the building and equipment $91,678 for a total of $126,678. After urging from the Carnegie Committee, the architect proposed such cost reductions as using white brick for stone at the rear facade, an iron grill instead of bronze and painted tin instead of copper.

Current Information: This is the Park Slope Branch of the Brooklyn Public Library. Current projects include roof work, air conditioning system upgrade, fence repair and general interior improvements.

Red Hook Branch Library, Exterior, n.d., c. 1915–1925, L.H. Dreyer Photographer;
Interior, n.d., c. 1915–25, (Brooklyn Public Library – Brooklyn Collection)

RED HOOK BRANCH

Address VISITATION PLACE & RICHARD STREET
Borough BROOKLYN
Date 1915
Architect RICHARD A. WALKER

Description: The library site was surrounded by a simple iron fence set into masonry pillars. There was a small lawn around the structure, with hedges planted in front of the facade.

The two story, three bay Mediterranean Revival style building was the only Brooklyn Carnegie designed in this style. The center entrance was arched, with a large cartouche above the doorway. The roof was the predominant feature of the building, with its balustrade, large bracketed overhanging eaves and deep cornice frieze pierced by attic windows. The architect, Richard A. Walker, joined the firm of Warren & Wetmore in 1915, before the library was completed.   The builder was John T. Brady & Company, which was also responsible for the Brownsville and Fort Hamilton Carnegie branches, both designed by Lord & Hewlett. The interior had decorative wooden staircases leading up to the mezzanine level and hanging light fixtures.

Notes: The library officially opened on April 22, 1915. John Devoy, Treasurer of the Carnegie Committee, presented the library to Lewis H. Pounds, Brooklyn Borough President representing New York City and to Horace J. Morse, representing the Brooklyn Public Library. There were addresses by W. Fred Silleck, Raymond V. Ingersoll and David Boody, President of the Carnegie Committee.   The site cost $10,500, the total cost was reported by the Brooklyn Public Library as $57,023. The Board of Estimate appropriated $10,000 for books in 1914.

Current Information: The Red Hook Branch library closed in August, 1946 after having been extensively damaged by a fire the year before. The property was surrendered to the City in 1947 and was demolished some time after that. The Red Hook Branch occupied space in other buildings until a new branch was built in 1975 at Wolcott and Dwight Streets.

Saratoga Branch Library, Exterior, 1994, Lisa Clifford, DGS Photographer; Interior, n.d., c. 1908, The Walter Studio, (Brooklyn Public Library – Brooklyn Collection)

SARATOGA BRANCH

Address	8 HOPKINSON AVENUE
Borough	BROOKLYN
Date	1908
Architect	R. L. DAUS OF DAUS & OTTO

Description: The library is located just off a major commercial street in a residential neighborhood. The neighborhood is made up of late 19th and early 20th century, three to six story brick buildings. Saratoga Square Park is nearby. There are highrise housing projects two blocks away. The building sits on a corner plot with a small lawn around the building. A simple, later-than-original iron fence defines the site and a modern ramp provides access to patrons.

The one story, seven bay red brick library has a stone base and stone door and window trim. There is foliate stone carving around the door. The projecting center entrance has a cartouche above the doorway. The Classical Revival library has a Spanish tile roof. The librarian complained of roof leaks shortly after the building was finished. The builder was W. L. Crow Construction Company, which also built the Walt Whitman Carnegie branch for R. L. Daus. The 10,000 square foot plus interior is light and airy, with paneled columns and the original ornate iron railing at the stacks. The hanging light fixtures have been replaced with fluorescents. The original ceiling has a simple cove molding. The original wood and glass vestibule screen has survived although the bronze dedication plaque, still found in most of the Carnegies, disappeared just prior to the major renovation.

There is a modern entrance door with an exterior roll down gate. The transom has been filled in with marble. Interior roll-down gates have been installed at the windows. There is a later second story rear addition. The library was rehabilitated in 1958-60. In 1974 the mechanical and heating, ventilation and air conditioning systems were upgraded.

Notes: The library officially opened on September 3, 1908. David A. Boody, President of the Carnegie Committee, presided over the ceremony. Acting Mayor Patrick McGowan and Roscoe Brown of the Brooklyn Public Library gave addresses. The branch replaced a branch library on Putnam Avenue, established in 1902 *Brooklyn Eagle* (3/6/1903). The site cost $24,751 and the building and equipment $48,034, for a total of $72,785.

Current Information: This is the Saratoga Branch of the Brooklyn Public Library. A full exterior and interior rehabilitation, including the installation of new exterior lighting and provisions for handicapped accessibility, was completed by Kaminsky, Wallace Architects in 1993.

South Branch Library, Exterior, n.d., c.1905; Interior, n.d., c. 1905,
(Brooklyn Public Library – Brooklyn Collection)

SOUTH BRANCH

Address	SOUTH WEST CORNER OF FOURTH AVENUE & 51ST STREET
Borough	BROOKLYN
Date	1905
Architects	LORD & HEWLETT

Description: This library was located on a corner lot and surrounded by a small lawn. Several letters were written to the Carnegie Committee suggesting other neighborhood locations, but the site originally picked by the agent for the committee was the final site.

The two story, five bay Classical Revival style building was brick with modest stone trim. Brick pilasters separated the multi-paned windows and the stone-trimmed center entrance. A high brick balustrade with attic windows rose above the dentillated cornice. The builder was the Church Construction Company which was also responsible for the Pacific and Park Slope Carnegie branches, designed by Raymond Almirall. The roof was repaired in 1949.

Notes: The library officially opened on December 9, 1905, with David A. Boody, President of the Carnegie Committee, presiding. The site cost $9,000 while the building and equipment cost $88,477, for a total of $97,477. The building was razed in 1970 and a new library was constructed on the same site.

Current Information: This branch was demolished in 1970 and a new branch was built. The new library is called the Sunset Park Branch of the Brooklyn Public Library, and is located at 5108 Fourth Avenue.

Stone Avenue Branch Library, Exterior, 1994, Lisa Clifford, DGS Photographer;
Interior, n.d., c. 1905, (Brooklyn Public Library – Brooklyn Collection)

STONE AVENUE BRANCH

Address	581 STONE AVENUE
Borough	BROOKLYN
Date	1914
Architect	WILLIAM B. TUBBY

Description: Once located in a residential neighborhood filled with low rise, late 19th and early 20th century houses, today the library is surrounded by Post-World War II high-rise housing projects. There is a public school nearby. The building is located on a corner site, taking up the full site and built to the building line. There is a simple, later iron fence surrounding the site.

The two story Jacobethan style brick building is different from the other Brooklyn Carnegies, with two entrances at the projecting corner tower, rather than a center entrance. There are large, multi-paned windows on each facade. An early or original elevation shows a more typical one story, three bay structure with a center entrance, but apparently this was not built. The builder was the firm of F. J. Kelly's Sons. The firm also built the DeKalb and Leonard Brooklyn Carnegie libraries, also for William Tubby. The interior has a two story high central space. The furniture was provided by Merritt & Company. There was Rookwood tile noted in specifications for the interior. This might be the tile at the fireplace surround. Designed especially for children, this library has a very embracing scale and some beautiful details. Original benches with carved rabbits still exist to delight the children of the 21st century.

The doors have been replaced and plaques between the first and second floors have been plastered over. Fluorescent lighting has been added to the interior. The building was rehabilitated in 1953-5. The roof was upgraded in 1976 and in 1994.

Notes: This was originally the Brownsville Children's Library, opened to relieve the crowding at the Brownsville Library, which itself was enlarged even before it opened in 1908. The Brownsville Children's Library was officially opened on September 24, 1914. Clara W. Hunt, the first branch librarian, was directly involved in the planning and the decision to make this library a specialized children's branch. The site cost $15,000 and the total cost was reported by the Brooklyn Public Library as $87,206.

Current Information: This is the Stone Avenue Branch of the Brooklyn Public Library. Plams are being developed by Rogers Marvel Architects to make the library accessible to the disabled.

Walt Whitman Branch Library, Exterior, 1994, Lisa Clifford, DGS Photographer; Interior, n.d., c. 1908–15, F.A. Walter Photographer, (Brooklyn Public Library – Brooklyn Collection)

WALT WHITMAN BRANCH

Address   ST. EDWARDS STREET & AUBURN PLACE
Borough   BROOKLYN
Date   1908
Architect R. L. DAUS OF DAUS & OTTO

Description: The library, once located in a residential neighborhood of low-rise houses, is now surrounded by high-rise housing projects. There is a school next door. The building sits on a corner lot and is surrounded by a lawn. The original iron fence around the site was lower than the present fence, but is similar in style, with simple slim vertical elements. A new section of railing has been added to the entrance.

The two story, three bay Classical Revival style building is red brick with limestone trim and an asphalt hipped roof. The projecting center entrance has a decorative, foliated stone surround topped by a cartouche. There are triple windows on the either side of the door. The builder was William L. Crow Construction Company, which also built the Saratoga Carnegie library, designed by the same architect. The austere 7,000 square foot interior has two story wooden stacks with the original decorative railing. The delivery desk has been moved to a side location.

The entrance door and the windows have been replaced and the transom over the door has been filled in with marble. There are modern fluorescent lights in the interior and a modern vestibule replaces the original one. The lamp posts on either side of the entrance have been removed. The library was rehabilitated in 1958-60.

Notes: This library was originally called the City Park Branch. It was renamed in 1943 for the Brooklyn poet Walt Whitman on the 125th anniversary of his birth. The library officially opened on September 1, 1908. David A. Boody, President of the Carnegie Committee, presented the library to the City. Arthur Somers, member of the Board of Education accepted the building for the City (*Brooklyn Citizen* 9/2/1908). Muller's orchestra provided the music, for this opening and nearly all of the rest. The library replaced an earlier City Park storefront branch (*Brooklyn Eagle* 12/15/1901). The site cost $59,600 and the building and equipment $41,855 for a total cost of $101,455.

Current Information: This is the Walt Whitman Branch of the Brooklyn Public Library. Current projects include access and security improvements to be designed by Allanbrook Benic Czajka Architects.

Washington Irving Branch Library, Exterior, 1994, Lisa Clifford, DGS Photographer; Interior, n.d., c. 1955, Frank Pearsall Photographer, (Brooklyn Public Library – Brooklyn Collection)

WASHINGTON IRVING BRANCH

Address	360 IRVING AVENUE
Borough	BROOKLYN
Date	1923
Architect	EDWARD L. TILTON

Description: The library is located on a busy residential and commercial street near Bushwick High School in a residential neighborhood of two to three story 20th century masonry houses. The building is situated on a corner lot, with a lawn in front. The site is enclosed by a simple iron fence.

This was the last Brooklyn Carnegie library built, designed not by the original five architects but by another architect, Edward Tilton. Edward Tilton was a library specialist who was highly regarded by James Bertram of the Carnegie Corporation. Tilton might have been involved with James Bertram's important 1911 publication on library design (*Notes on the Erection of Library Bildings [sic]*). The builder was the F.G. Fearon Company, which filed for bankruptcy before the building was finished.

The Tudor Revival two story, five bay red brick library has a projecting entrance with a gabled slate roof. The doorway is marked by a flat Elizabethan arch, the multi-paned windows are trimmed in stone. The 9,000 plus square foot interior is simple, with oak paneling and an original mantel. The delivery desk is located to one side. The original hanging incandescent lights have been replaced by fluorescent fixtures. The entrance door has been replaced on this largely intact building. The library was rehabilitated in 1960-3.

Notes: The library was officially opened on May 16, 1923. The Muller Music orchestra faithfully played at the opening, as they had for most of the Brooklyn Carnegie openings since 1906. The building was presented to the City by David Boody, President of the Carnegie Committee, and accepted by the Honorable Francis P. Bent, representative for the Mayor. There were speeches by Jared J. Chambers and the Reverend John L. York. The cost of the building was reported by the Brooklyn Public Library as $62,370. This library replaced the old Ridgewood branch library.

Current Information: This is the Washington Irving Branch of the Brooklyn Public Library. Current plans call for modifications to make the library accessible to the handicapped, and for security improvements.

Williamsburgh Branch Library, Exterior, 1994, Lisa Clifford, DGS Photographer; Interior, n.d., c. 1955, Frank Pearsall Photographer, Brooklyn Public Library – Brooklyn Collection

WILLIAMSBURGH BRANCH

Address   226-246 DIVISION AVENUE
Borough   BROOKLYN
Date   1905
Architects   RICHARD A. WALKER/WALKER & MORRIS

Description: The library is in a busy mixed residential and commercial area, on a street over the Brooklyn Queens Expressway. A school building and a former YMCA are nearby. The building is located on an unusual, almost-triangular shaped site, surrounded by a lawn. The site is enclosed by a simple iron fence which might be original; an extra section has been added to the entrance.

The two story red brick Classical Revival style library is eleven bays wide. It was the largest of the Carnegies when it was built. The center entrance is marked by contrasting quoins and a tall arched doorway. Side wings project at an angle from the entrance while the rear is semi-circular. The builder was the Remington Construction Company. The large 26,000 plus square foot interior has a central delivery desk with a the semicircular, two story stack section with original railings. The dramatic space has wood wainscoting and original mantels in the reading rooms.

The architect Richard A. Walker explained his design philosophy in 1903 when he responded to criticism about the placement and simplicity of the entrance (*Brooklyn Times* 1/28/03). "We considered the matter of the location of the entrance seriously and found none so advantageous as the one published last night. You will see from the ground floor plan that on entering one comes to the very centre of the property, and from there the librarian or person at the desk controls all the different rooms. This makes great economy in the administration of the library, reducing the number of necessary watchers and ensuring the greatest protection to the books. It seems to me that this is the first question to consider, the economy of administration and the simple and complete supervision of the entire first floor by one person."

The entrance door has been replaced and grates have been added to the windows. There is a later vestibule at the entrance. The library was rehabilitated in 1953-5, a period of intensive renovation for Brooklyn's libraries.

Notes: This was considered the first Brooklyn Carnegie library and the cornerstone laying ceremony in 1903 was a major one. Mayor Seth Low spoke to thousands, who gathered on the cold November day to participate in the event. The cornerstone contained the latest public library catalog; a copy of theCarnegie contract; copies of Brooklyn newspapers, and other documents.The site cost $84,461 and the building and equipment $115,389 for a total cost of $199,850. The Bedford and Williamsburgh Branches were featured in the March, 1903 *Library Journal* article favorably commenting on their planning and design.

Current Information: This is the Williamsburgh Branch of the Brooklyn Public Library. When the library was officially opened on January 28, 1905, its name was spelled "Williamsburg."

INVENTORY OF CARNEGIE LIBRARIES OF NEW YORK CITY

THE NEW YORK PUBLIC LIBRARY

THE BRONX

Riverdale ●

Edenwald ●

Woodlawn Heights ●

Wakefield/CRW ●

Van Cortlandt ●

Baychester ●

City Island ●

Spuyten Duyvil ●

Eastchester ●

Mosholu ●

Kingsbridge ● ☆

Allerton ●

Pelham Bay ●

Jerome Park ●

Van Nest ●

Fordham/CRW /Bronx Reference ★

Belmont ●

West Farms ●

Westchester Square ●

Francis Martin /CRW ●

Parkchester ●

Throg's Neck ●

★ *Tremont*

Clason's Point ●

Sedgwick ●

Castle Hill ●

Grand Concourse ●

Soundview ●

☆ ● High Bridge

★ *Morrisannia*

Woodstock ★

★ *Melrose*

★ *Hunt's Point*

★
Mott Haven/CRW

The New York
Public Library 1996

★ *Operating Carnegie Libraries*

☆ *Former Carnegie Libraries or sites*

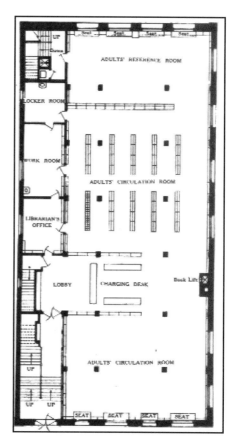

Fordham Branch Borough Library Center, Exterior,
1993, Lisa Clifford, DGS Photographer;
First Floor Plan in the Bulletin of the New York Public Library,
April 24 v. 28,
(Archives of The New York Public Library Astor,
Lenox and Tilden Foundations).

FORDHAM BRANCH

Address 2556 BAINBRIDGE AVENUE
Borough BRONX
Date 1923
Architects McKIM, MEAD & WHITE

Description: The library is located on a corner site. The Georgian Revival style Harvard-brick-faced building has, characteristically, an entrance at the side bay. The two story library has modest Indiana limestone trim primarily at the door, windows and cornice. The arched ground floor openings on the main, Bainbridge Avenue, facade are raised on a brick base. Corner brick quoins end in paneled stone capitals. The library was expanded with a new wing and second story addition in 1955, designed by Samuel J. Kessler & Sons, Architects. The builder was the William L. Crow Construction Company, who also built the Fort Washington, Mott Haven, Saratoga, 67th Street, and Walt Whitman New York City Carnegie Branches.

Notes: The library officially opened on September 22, 1923. The total cost of the site, building, and equipment including books was $186,500. The opening ceremony took place in nearby Poe Park. Two bands played as the members of the community and the library officials marched to the library two blocks away.

Current Information: This is the Fordham Library Center, the Bronx Borough library center and reference library of The New York Public Library. Current plans call for the replication of original wood windows and entrance door, designed by Sen Architects.

High Bridge Branch Library, Exterior and Interior, April 1933, Wurts Brothers Photographers, (Archives of The New York Public Library Astor, Lenox and Tilden Foundations).

HIGH BRIDGE BRANCH

Address   78 WEST 168TH STREET
Borough   BRONX
Date   1908
Architects   CARRERE & HASTINGS

Description: The library, which is no longer standing, was located on a corner site, with land around it and a lawn in front. The two story brick and Indiana limestone Classical Revival style library had a center entrance with a portico and arched upper floor windows. The red cedar shingle hipped roof had overhanging eaves. There was approximately 8,000 square feet of interior space. The builder was John T. Brady & Company, who also worked with Carrere & Hastings, Architects on the Hamilton Fish Park and Hudson Park Carnegie Branches.

Notes: The library officially opened on July 22, 1908. The site cost $16,000 and the building and equipment $34,556 for a total of $50,556. A branch library funded by public spirited citizens was operating in the neighborhood for five years previous to the opening of the Carnegie branch.

Current Information: The High Bridge Branch of The New York Public Library was replaced by a new library on the same site in the 1970's.

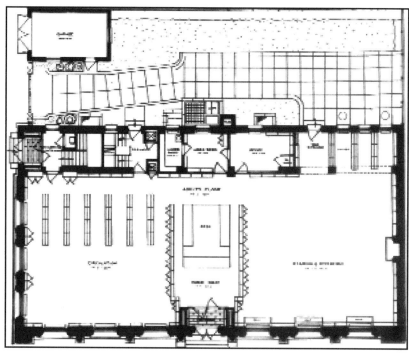

Hunt's Point Branch Regional Library, Exterior, 1993, Lisa Clifford, DGS Photographer; First Floor Plan in the Bulletin of The New York Public Library, June 1930, v. 34, (The New York Public Library Astor, Lenox and Tilden Foundations).

HUNT'S POINT BRANCH

Address	877 SOUTHERN BOULEVARD
Borough	BRONX
Date	1929
Architects	CARRERE & HASTINGS

Description: The library is located on a corner site on busy, wide Southern Boulevard and is built to the building line. The nine story Erma Cava Houses for the Elderly is located next door. The neighborhood is made up of five and six story early 20th century brick tenements and modern low rise public housing.

The two story brick building with stone and terra cotta trim is seven bays wide with an entrance in the center bay. The ground floor is made up of a series of arches with deeply recessed door and windows. The design was noted in The New York Public Library *Bulletin* (June, 1930) as 14th century Florentine. The architects, Carrere & Hastings, designed more Carnegie Branches than any other firm. The builder, the E.E. Paul Company, built the Stapleton, Tottenville, Port Richmond, Epiphany, Riverside, Muhlenberg, and Woodstock Carnegie Branches for Carrere & Hastings, Architects and the 58th Street Branch for Babb, Cook & Willard. This was the latest New York City Carnegie Branch built, and in keeping with the new automotive era, included an adjacent one story garage for The Bronx Book Wagon.

On the exterior the original windows have been replaced with modern aluminum sash but the wood paneled door with an upper glass panel covered by a decorative metal grille is early or original. On the inside, there is a wood paneled vestibule, high plaster ceilings and original molding. The approximately six foot high wood shelving on the perimeter and the free-standing book cases are early or original. Alterations include linoleum flooring and fluorescent lighting replacing the original pendant fixtures. There was repair and renovation work on the building as early as 1939.

Notes: The library was officially opened for book circulation on July 1, 1929. It was built with unexpended funds from the Carnegie account. The total cost was $151,875. It was the thirty-ninth and last of The New York Public Library branches built with Carnegie funds.

Current Information: This is the Hunt's Point Regional Library of The New York Public Library.

Kingsbridge Branch Library, Exterior, 1993, Lisa Clifford, DGS Photographer.

KINGSBRIDGE BRANCH

Address   3041 KINGSBRIDGE AVENUE
Borough   BRONX
Date   1905
Architects   McKIM, MEAD & WHITE

Description: The library building, now a nursery school, is located in the middle of the block front, deeply set back on a large plot of land and flanked by two early 20th century churches. An iron fence shared with the Episcopal Church of the Mediator divides the front of the property from the sidewalk.

The one story, three bay brick neo-Federal style building has splayed stone lintels characteristic of the style. The over-sized pedimented entrance had multi-paned side-lights and transom surrounding the door, now filled in. The simple interior was originally approximately 3700 square feet. It has been altered to accommodate the school, but a number of original features remain, including the original plaster ceiling with cornice molding and the window trim. The builder was Michael Reid & Company, who worked with McKim, Mead & White on all but two of their Carnegie branches. The McKim, Mead & White/Michael Reid Company Carnegie branches are: Chatham Square; 125th Street; 135th Street; Rivington; Kingsbridge; St. Gabriel's Park; Tompkins Square; Hamilton Grange; and Harlem.

Notes: The library was officially opened on May 19, 1905. The land was given to The New York Public Library by Mr. and Mrs. James Douglass, for $1. The building and equipment cost $22,821.

Current Information: The Kingsbridge Branch of The New York Public Library was decommissioned in 1958. A new branch was built at 280 West 231st Street. The old Carnegie branch building still serves a community function and is now the Spuyten Duyvil Infantry and Preschool.

Melrose Branch Library, Exterior, 1993, Lisa Clifford, DGS Photographer.

MELROSE BRANCH

Address 910 MORRIS AVENUE
Borough BRONX
Date 1914
Architects CARRERE & HASTINGS

Description: The library is located on a corner lot in a busy commercial and residential neighborhood of 20th century low and mid-rise buildings. It is built to the building line.

The original library was a brick building with limestone trim and a granite base. While the two story brick building on the site today appears to be a modern 1950's structure, it is apparently an extensively rehabilitated original Carnegie branch. The upper floors of the originally nearly 29,000 square foot building were removed to create an approximately 9,000 square foot structure. The windows were replaced and the openings apparently changed. The facade appears to have been refaced. There were extensive interior alterations as well. The architects, Carrere & Hastings, designed thirteen Carnegie branches, the most of any of the architects involved. They were also responsible for the main New York Public Library at 42nd Street. This was the only Carnegie branch for the builder, Edwin Outwater. The architects of the 1950's rehabilitation, Bloch & Hesse, worked on other libraries in the 1950's.

Notes: The Melrose Branch was officially opened on January 14, 1914. The cost of the site was $20,000 and the building and equipment $102,974, for a total of $122,974. Extensive renovations costing more than $200,000, were finished in 1959.

Current Information: This is the Melrose Branch of The New York Public Library. Current plans include upgrading of the air conditioning system and roof replacement.

Morrisiana Branch Library, Exterior, 1993, Lisa Clifford, DGS Photographer,
Exterior, n.d.c. 1908, Wurts Brothers Photographers
(Archives of The New York Public Library Astor, Lenox and Tilden Foundations.)

MORRISANIA BRANCH

Address   610 EAST 169TH STREET
Borough BRONX
Date   1908
Architects BABB, COOK & WILLARD

Description: The library is located at a crossroads across from McKinley Square. The immediate neighborhood is residential, with stores at the ground floors of the predominantly early to mid-20th century low and mid-rise brick tenements. Claremont Village, the largest housing project in New York City, lies two blocks away at Third Avenue. The branch serves the entire Morrisania community. The library is next to a junior high school. There are small lawns in front of the two wings, fenced with the original iron rail and stone pillars.

The two story, five bay Classical Revival style brick building has Indiana limestone trim and a pink Milford granite base. The two, two-story wings are lower and recessed from the main facade. There is a projecting stone entrance bay with a large decorative panel featuring the New York City shield above. The builder was Richard Deeves & Son, who also built the Seward Park Carnegie Branch for Babb, Cook & Welch, Architects.

There is a later entrance door and modern aluminum windows with mesh grilles at the first floor. There are a number of original features inside the approximately 14,000 square foot building. The existing large superintendent's apartment will soon be converted to staff office space. There is a wood paneled vestibule, original bookshelves, original stair at the rear and original rectangular plaster faced columns with molded capitals. The ceiling has been dropped in sections, but the original beams are visible along the edges. There are modern fluorescent hanging fixtures, and modern linoleum flooring.

Notes: Originally called the McKinley Square Branch, the library was officially opened on December 1, 1908. The site cost $48,500 and the building and equipment $108,482 for a total of $156,982. The branch was actively sought after by residents of the neighborhood: hundreds of people signed petitions for a branch.

Current Information: This is the Morrisania Branch of The New York Public Library. The extensive rehabilitation work, which will begin in 1995, includes reorganization of ground floor spaces and upgrading of finishes, woodwork, lighting and heating, ventilation and air conditioning systems. The projects architects, DCI International, received an Art Commission award for design excellence for their efforts to make the entire building handicapped accessible.

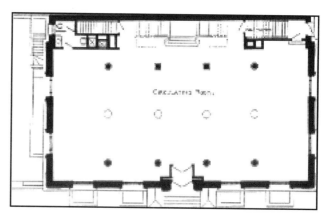

Mott Haven Branch Library, Exterior, 1993, Lisa Clifford,
DGS Photographer; First Floor Plan in T.W. Koch, A
Portfolio of Carnegie Libraries, 1907.

MOTT HAVEN BRANCH

Address	321 EAST 140TH STREET
Borough	BRONX
Date	1905
Architects	CARRERE & HASTINGS

Description: The library is located on a corner site within the Mott Haven Historic District, surrounded by notable 19th century row houses. The library is built to the building line.

The ornate Classical Revival style three story, five bay brick building has lavish Indiana limestone trim. The stone trim tooling was specified at 8 cuts to the inch, a characteristic of many of the other Carnegies. There is a center entrance marked by blocks, which are repeated as stone quoins at the corners. The pedimented windows are arched on the ground floor and rectangular above. There is a prominent modillioned cornice. The builder was William L. Crow, who also built the 67th Street Carnegie Branch for Babb, Cook & Willard, Architects and the Brooklyn Saratoga and Walt Whitman Carnegie Branches for Daus & Otto, Architects.

The library is largely intact, with wood sash windows in the same fenestration pattern as the originals. Wood panels under the windows on the front facade probably mark the removal of iron balconies like those on the side facade. On the inside, the approximately 15,000 square foot space is partly intact. Outstanding early or original features include the wood window trim, round and rectangular columns with simple molded capitals, freestanding wood paneled vestibule, large round cast iron heater, and an elegant staircase with a decorative iron railing. The original skylight exists but has been covered over, and the original high plaster ceiling has been partly obscured with a later dropped ceiling.

Notes: The library officially opened on March 31, 1905. The site cost $22,500 and the building and equipment $96,796 for a total of $119,296. As with all of the Carnegie branches, there was a live-in custodian through at least the 1960's. In 1949 the advertised salary was $60.83 a month and a 5 room apartment.

Current Information: This is the Mott Haven Branch of The New York Public Library. The library is located within the New York City Mott Haven Historic District and the Mott Haven National Register Historic District. Current plans by Cabrera Barricklo Architects, PC include a new roof, restoration of original wooden windows and doors, select masonry repointing, masonry cleaning and plumbing and heating, ventilation, and air conditioning system work.

Tremont Branch Library, Exterior, 1993, Lisa Clifford, DGS Photographer; Interior Renovation, 1949 (Department of General Services).

TREMONT BRANCH

Address   1866 WASHINGTON AVENUE
Borough   BRONX
Date   1905
Architects CARRERE & HASTINGS

Description: The library is located on a corner site in a residential neighborhood a block from a busy commercial street. The surrounding buildings are an eclectic mix of later 19th and 20th century primarily masonry structures from one to six stories high. A small Queen Anne style house is adjacent to the library.

The two story, originally five bay neo-Federal style library has a simple center entrance. A sixth bay, slightly recessed from the main facade but matching in color and style, was added in 1915-6. It was built with left-over Carnegie funds. The facade is red brick laid up in a Flemish bond and Indiana limestone trim. The tall ground floor keystone-arched windows match the doorway, the upper windows are rectangular with iron balconies. The facade is topped by a molded stone cornice below a brick and stone parapet. The builder was John V. Schaefer, Jr., who also built the Bushwick Carnegie Branch Library in Brooklyn for Raymond Almirall, Architect.

The library is largely intact. A roll-down gate has been installed at the entrance door. On the approximately 12,000 square foot interior, there is a paneled wooden vestibule with a transom and several paneled oak and glass partitions. The original high plaster beamed ceiling has been lowered in part and the fluorescent lighting is modern. The wood window trim and round columns with molded capitals are original.

Notes: There was a cornerstone laying ceremony on January 21, 1904 attended by several hundred people. The Reverend F. B. Makepeace, President of the Bronx Free Library, spoke about the history of the Bronx Free Library, which had just merged with The New York Public Library. The library officially opened on July 22, 1905. The ceremonies were held in the library's assembly room. The Reverend Makepeace spoke, along with Arthur Bostwick, Chief of the Circulation Department and William Harman Black, Commissioner of Accounts and representative of the Mayor. When it opened, the building had a staff of nine and accommodations for a custodian. *New York Times* (7/23/1905, 12:6) The site cost $18,750 and the building and equipment $81,926 for a total of $100,676. The population of the neighborhood increased so dramatically after the library was built that an addition was built in 1915-16 using surplus funds from the Carnegie bequest.

Current Information: This is the Tremont Branch of The New York Public Library. Current plans include waterproofing, drainage and replacement in kind of the original wood windows, designed by Ralph Sobel Architect. Future plans by Sen Architects include compliance with the Americans with Disabilities Act and select interior renovation.

Woodstock Branch Library, Exterior, 1993, Lisa Clifford, DGS Photographer; Interior n.d.,
c. 1914, (Archives of the New York Public Library Astor, Lenox and Tilden Foundations)

WOODSTOCK BRANCH

Address   761 EAST 160TH STREET
Borough   BRONX
Date   1914
Architects   McKIM, MEAD & WHITE

Description: The library is located in the middle of the block front and built to the building line. It is in a residential neighborhood of modern two story public housing and early 20th century five and six story brick tenements. There is a public school across the street.

The three story, three bay Classical Revival style library is faced in rusticated Indiana limestone. This treatment is typical of the architects, McKim, Mead & White. There are arched windows on the first and second floors and rectangular on the third. The builder, the E.E. Paul Company, built the Stapleton, Tottenville, Port Richmond, Epiphany, Riverside, Muhlenberg Carnegie Branches for Carrere & Hastings, Architects and the 58th Street Branch for Babb, Cook & Willard.

The window and door openings were made smaller in 1966-8, with the arches filled in at the top. A new entrance door and multi-paned windows were installed in the openings.   The two center windows have been blocked up entirely. The interior, including all of the mechanical systems, was renovated in 1966-8. The approximately 16,500 square foot interior today has the original high plaster ceiling with simple molded cornice. There has been a change in plan, with a new entrance vestibule, stairs, and new hallway partitions.

Notes: The library officially opened on February 17, 1914. The site cost $14,000 and the building and equipment $116,760 for a total of $130,760.

Current Information: This is the Woodstock Branch of The New York Public Library. Current plans by The Stephen B. Jacobs Group call for new windows and an entrance door which recall the original design.

INVENTORY OF CARNEGIE LIBRARIES OF NEW YORK CITY

THE NEW YORK PUBLIC LIBRARY

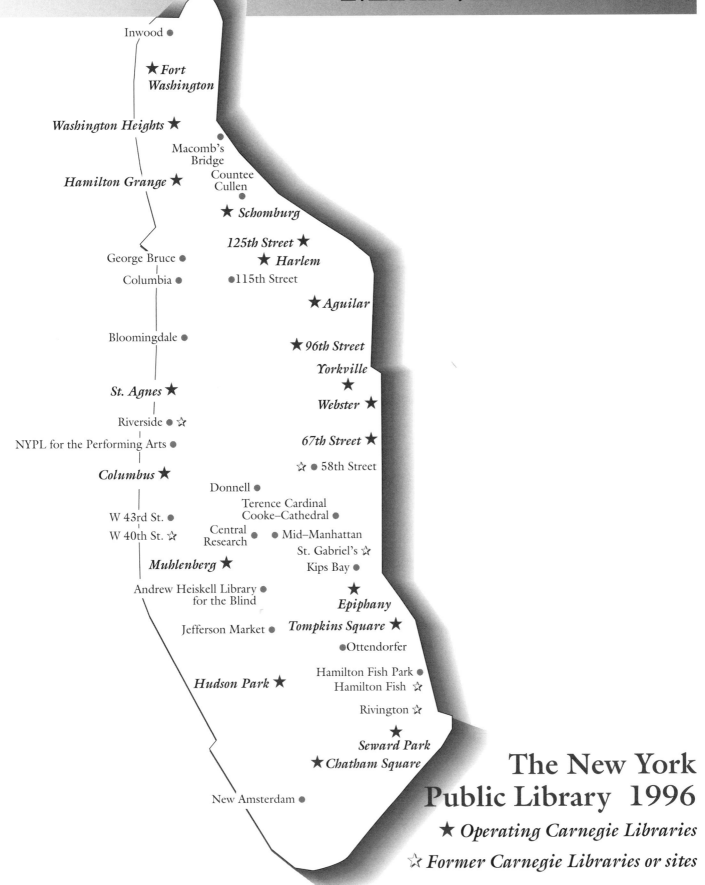

MANHATTAN

Inwood ●

★ *Fort Washington*

Washington Heights ★

Macomb's Bridge ●

Hamilton Grange ★

Countee Cullen ●

★ *Schomburg*

125th Street ★

George Bruce ●

★ *Harlem*

Columbia ●

●115th Street

★ *Aguilar*

Bloomingdale ●

★ *96th Street*

Yorkville ★

St. Agnes ★

Webster ★

Riverside ● ☆

NYPL for the Performing Arts ●

67th Street ★

☆ ● 58th Street

Columbus ★

Donnell ●

W 43rd St. ●

Terence Cardinal Cooke–Cathedral ●

W 40th St. ☆

Central Research ●

● Mid–Manhattan

St. Gabriel's ☆

Muhlenberg ★

Kips Bay ●

Andrew Heiskell Library for the Blind ●

★

Epiphany

Jefferson Market ●

Tompkins Square ★

●Ottendorfer

Hamilton Fish Park ●

Hudson Park ★

Hamilton Fish ☆

Rivington ☆

★

Seward Park

★ *Chatham Square*

New Amsterdam ●

The New York Public Library 1996

★ *Operating Carnegie Libraries*

☆ *Former Carnegie Libraries or sites*

*Aguilar Branch Library, Exterior, 1993, Lisa Clifford, DGS Photographer;
First Floor Renovation, 1951 (Department of General Services).*

AGUILAR BRANCH

Address   172-4 EAST 110TH STREET
Borough   MANHATTAN
Date   1905
Architects HERTS & TALLANT

Description: The library is located in the middle of the block front in a densely populated neighborhood in East Harlem. The low-rise structures on the street have commercial ground floors with residential use above. The library extends to the building line.

The unusual three story Classical Revival style building has two oversized, full height Indiana limestone Doric columns at either end of the facade. The columns rest on a high projecting Maine granite base. They support a large projecting limestone cornice with a carved frieze featuring classical figures and foliation. The windows are separated by metal spandrels and by slim metal Corinthian columns. This was the only Carnegie branch library designed by Herts & Tallant, who apparently were the architects for the first building in 1899. The builders, General Building and Construction, also built just one Carnegie branch. This library is apparently not an entirely new building but is rather an extensive renovation of the earlier Aguilar Library building on the same site.

The entrance door and the windows have been replaced. A mesh security grille has been added to the first floor windows. The approximately 13,000 square foot building had major renovations in 1939, 1950 and 1995.

Notes: The Aguilar Branch officially opened on November 29, 1905. Part of the site was donated by the Aguilar Free Library Society. The remainder of the site cost $14,070 while the building and equipment cost $77,669, for a total of $91,739.

Current Information: This is the Aguilar Branch of The New York Public Library. A major interior and exterior renovation and restoration, including compliance with the Americans with Disabilities Act, was completed in 1996. The improvements are part of The New York Public Library's Adopt-A-Branch program and a part of the cost of renovation is being paid for with private funds. The architects were Gruzen Samton.

Chatham Square Branch Regional Library, Exterior, 1993, Lisa Clifford, DGS Photographer;
Interior, c. 1910, Lewis Hine Photographer
(Archives of The New York Public Library Astor, Lenox and Tilden Foundations).

CHATHAM SQUARE BRANCH

Address   33 EAST BROADWAY
Borough   MANHATTAN
Date   1903
Architects McKIM, MEAD & WHITE

Description: The library is located in the middle of the block front on a very busy two-way commercial street, East Broadway. The neighborhood is a densely populated commercial and residential area. The architecture is mixed, with four to twenty story masonry buildings dating from the 19th and 20th centuries. The monumental scale, in particular the oversized classical ornament, makes the building stand out in the neighborhood.

The spectacular, three story, three bay Classical Revival style building has dramatic two-story high arched openings at the rusticated stone base. A massive row of six Ionic columns at the upper stories add depth to the basically flat facade. The builder was Michael Reid & Company, who worked with McKim, Mead & White on all but two of their Carnegie branches. The McKim, Mead & White/Michael Reid Company Carnegie branches are: Chatham Square; 125th Street; 135th Street; Rivington; Kingsbridge; St. Gabriel's Park; Tompkins Square; Hamilton Grange; and Harlem.

The library is essentially intact, down to the original lanterns at the front door on the exterior. The windows and entrance door have been replaced. On the inside, the lighting, mechanical systems, charge desk, and floor covering have been replaced. There is a small wood paneled entrance vestibule and a paneled oak screen on the third floor. The original stair and decorative iron rail have survived. There are typical round Doric plaster columns on all floors. Originally, the first floor contained the children's reading room, with the adult reading rooms on the second and third floors. Today, the children's reading room is upstairs. A large meeting room with exposed ductwork was created on the third floor in the 1970's.

Notes: The Chatham Square Branch officially opened on November 2, 1903. The opening was held in the library's assembly room and attended by community members. Speakers included Dr. John S. Billings, Director of The New York Public Library, Manhattan Borough President Jacob Cantor, and Arthur Bostwick, Chairman of the Circulating Department of The New York Public Library. Mr. Bostwick spoke on the preferences of the Chatham Square community, which were for non-fiction. There had been a Chatham Square branch in a storefront at 22 East Broadway. When it opened, the library was run by a librarian and ten assistants. New York Times (11/3/1903, 14:3) The site cost $63,000 and the building and equipment $83,184, for a total of $146,184.

Current Information: This is the Chatham Square Branch of The New York Public Library. It functions as a Regional Library.

Columbus Branch Library, Exterior, 1993, Lisa Clifford, DGS Photographer; Interior, n.d., c. 1910
(Archives of The New York Public Library Astor, Lenox and Tilden Foundations)

COLUMBUS BRANCH

Address   742 TENTH AVENUE
Borough   MANHATTAN
Date   1909
Architects BABB, COOK & WILLARD

Description: The library is located in the middle of the block front on a busy commercial street of diverse 19th and 20th century masonry buildings of varying heights. The library is built to the building line.

The two story, three bay Renaissance Revival style building is faced in Indiana limestone over a Maine granite base. The building was originally three stories high, topped by a stone balustrade. The third floor was removed in 1960. The remaining facade has tall arched openings in a rusticated ground floor and rectangular second floor windows with imposing pediments. There was originally a roof garden, also known as an open-air reading room, which was used when the weather was warm. The entrance door and the windows have been replaced and one basement window and window well have been closed up. The architects were Babb, Cook & Willard, who also designed the Mott Haven, Morrisania, 96th Street, St. Agnes, Webster, and 58th Street Carnegies. The builder, the Thomas J. Brady Company, built just one Carnegie library.

The approximately 11,000 square foot interior has retained its high ceilings, which are now covered with later 20th century acoustical tile. The original staircase with its graceful iron railing has survived from the first to the second floor. There is an oak-paneled entrance vestibule.

Notes: The library officially opened on September 24, 1909. The site cost $37,427 and the building and equipment $119,324, for a total of $153,751.

Current Information: This is the Columbus Branch of The New York Public Library. Current plans by RB Consulting Engineer call for improved lighting which recalls the earlier pendant fixtures.

*Epiphany Branch Library, Exterior, 1993, Lisa Clifford, DGS Photographer;
First Floor Renovation, 1949 (Department of General Services).*

EPIPHANY BRANCH

Address   228-230 EAST 23RD STREET
Borough MANHATTAN
Date   1907
Architects CARRERE & HASTINGS

Description: The library is located on a wide, busy commercial street at the building line. The immediate neighborhood contains a mix of 20th century masonry buildings of all heights.

The three story, four bay (plus a smaller, recessed 1980's fifth bay) limestone building has tall keystone-arched openings on the ground floor. There is a ground floor cornice with a decorative frieze as well as a dentillated stone cornice at the roof. The upper floors have rectangular windows with bracketed, decorative pediments. The builder, the E.E. Paul Company, built the Stapleton, Tottenville, Port Richmond, Epiphany, Riverside, Muhlenberg Carnegie Branches for Carrere & Hastings, Architects, the Woodstock Branch for McKim, Mead & White, and the 58th Street Branch for Babb, Cook & Willard.

The over 10,000 square foot interior has the original staircase with its decorative iron rail, original high ceilings and rectangular columns. Changes include new lighting, a rear addition, and a modern glass block wall. The windows have been replaced, the entrance door has been turned into a window and the new entrance was moved to a 1980's side bay to provide for accessibility for the handicapped. Glass and Glass Architects were responsible for the design of the renovation. There was a major WPA-funded renovation in 1939. Plans for demolition in 1968 were successfully opposed by the community.

Notes: The library officially opened on September 20, 1907. The site cost $71,845 and the building and equipment $87,608, for a total of $159,453. The Friends of Epiphany Branch has over 250 members that support library projects.

Current Information: This is the Epiphany Branch of The New York Public Library. Current projects include the installation of a Building Management System and an initial survey for Americans with Disabilities Act improvements.

58th Street Branch Library, Exterior, 1928, Wurts Brothers Photographers; Interior, n.d., Schavendorf Photographer (Archives of The New York Public Library Astor, Lenox and Tilden Foundations).

58TH STREET BRANCH

Address   121-7 EAST 58TH STREET
Borough   MANHATTAN
Date   1907
Architects CARRERE & HASTINGS

Description: The library was situated in the middle of the block front in a residential neighborhood. It was built to the building line. The large, elaborate Renaissance Revival style stone building was four stories high and five bays wide. There were pedimented, arched entrances at each end on the rusticated stone ground floor. The second and third floor center windows were marked by pediments and the facade ended in a deep modillioned cornice. The builder, the E.E. Paul Company, built the Stapleton, Tottenville, Port Richmond, Epiphany, Riverside, Muhlenberg Carnegie Branches for Carrere & Hastings, Architects, the Woodstock Branch for McKim, Mead & White, and the 58th Street Branch for Babb, Cook & Willard.

Notes: The library officially opened on May 10, 1907. The site cost $89,000 and the building and equipment $119,245 for a total of $208,245.

Current Information: The 58th Street Branch was decommissioned by The New York Public Library and demolished. It was replaced by a new branch at 127 East 58th Street.

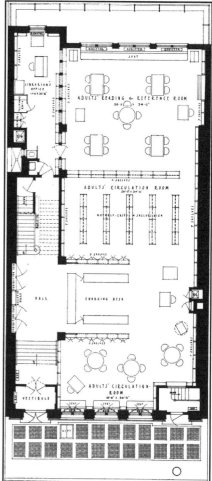

Fort Washington Branch Library,
Exterior, Lisa Clifford,
DGS Photographer;
First Floor Plan, n.d., c. 1914,
(Archives of the New York Public Library Astor,
Lenox and Tilden Foundations).

FORT WASHINGTON BRANCH

Address   535-7 WEST 179TH STREET
Borough   MANHATTAN
Date   1914
Architects   COOK & WELCH

Description: The library is located in the middle of the block front on a quiet, one way residential street. The surrounding architecture primarily consists of six story brick apartment buildings dating from the first half of the 20th century.

The three story, five bay Classical Revival style library has a graceful limestone facade with a rusticated ground floor and a granite base. The arched side door is balanced by another unused door on the other side. There is a set of three arched windows in the center of the first and second floors. There is a curved parapet above the modillioned stone cornice. There are small lanterns flanking the entrance door. The builder was the William S. Crow Construction Company, who also built the Saratoga and Walt Whitman Brooklyn Carnegie Branches for Daus & Otto, Architects.

The entrance door has been replaced. The wooden windows are original or replacements-in-kind. The skylight was replaced by concrete roof decking. The approximately 14,500 square foot interior is dominated by a mezzanine with early or original wooden stacks and a decorative metal balcony. There are rectangular plaster columns and a high plaster ceiling. Among the many early or original features are the wooden display case, wood paneling at entrance, stairs with decorative metal railing, wooden stacks, plaster ceiling and rectangular columns. There was a major renovation in 1950 after a fire in the basement.

Notes: The library officially opened on April 14, 1914. The site cost $20,000 and the building and equipment $112,607, for a total of $132,607.

Current Information: This is the Fort Washington Branch of The New York Public Library. The current project will incorporate a Building Management System to monitor and control energy usage for all basic building systems.

Hamilton Fish Park Branch Library,
Roof Garden and Interior View, c. 1910, Lewis Hine Photographer
(Archives of The New York Public Library Astor, Lenox and Tilden Foundations).

HAMILTON FISH BRANCH

Address   388-92 EAST HOUSTON STREET
Borough   MANHATTAN
Date   1906
Architects CARRERE & HASTINGS

Description: The library was located in the middle of the block front in a residential and commercial area. The three story, five bay red brick Classical Revival style building had an entrance at a side bay rather than in the center of the facade. Keystone-arched ground floor openings and arched second floor windows dominated the facade. There was a lower third floor above a dentillated cornice. A roof garden was open to readers in the warm weather, from about May to October. Over 16,000 people visited the roof garden when it was first opened to the public in 1909 New York Times (4/24/1910, 2). The builder was the John T. Brady Company, who also built the Hudson Park and High Bridge Carnegie Branches for Carrere & Hastings, Architects as well as the Brooklyn Brownsville and Fort Hamilton Carnegies for Lord & Hewlett and the Red Hook Carnegie Branch for Walker & Morris. The building contained approximately 17,000 square feet of space.

Notes: The library officially opened on February 26, 1909. The site cost $65,354 and the building and equipment $114,856, for a total of $180,210.

Current Information: The Hamilton Fish Branch was decommissioned in 1958 by The New York Public Library and is no longer standing. There is a public housing project in its place. The branch was replaced by a new, over 10,000 square foot, Hamilton Fish Park Branch at 415 East Houston Street in 1960.

Hamilton Grange Branch Library, Exterior, 1993, Lisa Clifford, DGS Photographer;
Interior n.d., c. 1907-1915
(Archives of The New York Public Library Astor, Lenox and Tilden Foundations).

HAMILTON GRANGE BRANCH

Address 503 WEST 145TH STREET
Borough MANHATTAN
Date 1907
Architects McKIM, MEAD & WHITE

Description: The library is located in the middle of the block front in a residential neighborhood of one to six story masonry buildings from the 19th and 20th centuries. P.S. 186 is located on the same block. The building is built to the building line. The front entrance steps have been removed but probably original lanterns have survived and the ornate cast iron fence is intact.

The elegant Renaissance Revival style building has a rusticated limestone facade with an arched center entrance flanked by tall arched windows with keystones of cherubs holding up books. The second floor window treatments are in characteristic Italian Renaissance style, with alternating arched and triangular pediments. There are also slim, narrow windows in between, undoubtedly to add more light to the reading room. The builder was Michael Reid & Company, who worked with McKim, Mead & White on all but two of their Carnegie branches. The McKim, Mead & White/Michael Reid Company Carnegie branches are: Chatham Square; 125th Street; 135th Street; Rivington; Kingsbridge; St. Gabriel's Park; Tompkins Square; Hamilton Grange; and Harlem.

On the exterior the entrance door has been replaced; the wood windows are early or original. The approximately 20,000 square foot interior has been altered over the years. There was a major rehabilitation in 1975. The vestibule is modern, the inside stairs have been replaced, an elevator has been installed, there are large fluorescent fixtures and a partially dropped ceiling.

Notes: The library officially opened on January 8, 1907. The site cost $44,602 and the building and equipment $110,682, for a total of $155,284.

Current Information: This is the Hamilton Grange Branch of The New York Public Library. The building is a designated New York City Landmark and listed on the National and State Registers of Historic Places. Current plans call for the rehabilitation of the ornamental iron fence and the addition of an architecturally sympathetic areaway grating by Cabrera Barricklo Architects and a partial interior renovation by Robert G. Neiley Architects.

Harlem Branch Library, Exterior, 1993, Lisa Clifford, DGS Photographer;
Interior, c. 1910, Lewis Hine Photographer
(Archives of The New York Public Library Astor, Lenox and Tilden Foundations).

HARLEM BRANCH

Address   9-11 WEST 124TH STREET
Borough   MANHATTAN
Date   1909
Architects McKIM, MEAD & WHITE

Description: The library is located in the middle of the block front in a residential neighborhood across from Marcus Garvey Park. The building is built to the building line, and projects slightly from the adjacent buildings, in particular from the 1940's brick convent next door.

The three story, three bay limestone over granite base Classical Revival style library has an entrance on the side rather than at the center bay. The tall arched openings are unusual in that they slope inward, making the windows and door recessed. The upper windows are separated by pilasters with Corinthian capitals. There are lanterns at the entrance. The builder was Michael Reid & Company, who worked with McKim, Mead & White on all but two of their Carnegie branches. The McKim, Mead & White/Michael Reid Company Carnegie branches are: Chatham Square; 125th Street; 135th Street; Rivington; Kingsbridge; St. Gabriel's Park; Tompkins Square; Hamilton Grange; and Harlem.

The entrance door and the windows have been replaced and the first floor windows have been shortened. A new roof was installed in 1981. The approximately 13,000 square foot interior contains a marble wainscoted vestibule with a wood and glass screen above. In the main reading room there is a great deal of wood paneling, a wood and glass display case, some early or original book cases. There is an original marble staircase with a decorative metal rail. There were rehabilitations in the 1930's and the 1950's.

Notes: The library officially opened on January 11, 1909. The site cost $60,000 and the building and equipment $93,544, for a total of $153,544.

Current Information: This is the Harlem Branch of The New York Public Library. The current 125th Street Carnegie Branch, opened in 1904, was initially called the Harlem Branch, but its name was changed after the branch library at 124th Street was opened five years later in 1909 as the Harlem Branch. Current plans include the upgrade of the heating, ventilation and air conditioning systems, an auditorium rehabilitation, fence work, and an Americans with Disabilities Act survey and initial compliance improvements.

Hudson Park Branch Library, 1993, Lisa Clifford, DGS Photographer;
Interior, c. 1910, Lewis Hine Photographer
(Archives of The New York Public Library Astor, Lenox and Tilden Foundations).

HUDSON PARK BRANCH

Address   66 LEROY STREET
Borough   MANHATTAN
Date   1906
Architects   CARRERE & HASTINGS

Description: This library is located in the middle of the block front on a busy street in Greenwich Village, just outside the Historic District. It is situated next to a community center and pool. Seventh Avenue South was cut through the area after the library was built, completely changing the immediate landscape and obliterating Hudson Park. Ironically, the presence of the park was the deciding factor in choosing the site. The modest brick two story building is now much smaller than its neighbors.

The main entrance for the brick Federal style library is on Leroy Street, in a three bay facade with arched openings and an entrance in one of the two side bays. The multi-paned windows have decorative transoms. There is a dentillated cornice below a brick parapet with stone insets. The builder was the John T. Brady Company, who also built the Hamilton Fish and High Bridge Carnegie Branches for Carrere & Hastings, Architects as well as the Brooklyn Brownsville and Fort Hamilton Carnegies for Lord & Hewlett and the Red Hook Carnegie Branch for Walker & Morris.

The over 15,000 square foot interior has original round plaster columns and simple wood window trim. There are partially lowered ceilings and modern fluorescent light fixtures. Major alterations in 1920 by Carrere & Hastings apparently involved extending the library to the newly cut through 7th Avenue South. There were also alterations in 1939.

Notes: The library officially opened on January 24, 1906. The site cost $44,000 and the building and equipment $78,894, for a total of $122,894.

Current Information: This is the Hudson Park Branch of The New York Public Library. Current projects include facade restoration by Rogers Marvel Architects and the installation of a Building Management System.

Muhlenberg Branch Library, Exterior, 1993, Lisa Clifford, DGS Photographer;
Interior, n.d., c. 1950, James W. Welgos Photographer
(Archives of The New York Public Library Astor, Lenox and Tilden Foundations).

MUHLENBERG BRANCH

Address	209-211 WEST 23RD STREET
Borough	MANHATTAN
Date	1906
Architects	CARRERE & HASTINGS

Description: The library is located on a busy commercial street, surrounded by a broad mix of masonry structures, primarily four story 19th century masonry row houses and six to ten story early 20th century brick apartment buildings. It is adjacent to the McBurney YMCA. The library is built to the building line.

The three story, three bay classical Renaissance Revival style structure has a limestone facade with tall, arched ground floor openings with carved keystones. The second floor windows are topped by pediments with ornamental carved stone friezes. There are bronze lanterns flanking the doorway. The library is very similar to the Epiphany Branch, another Carnegie designed by Carrere & Hastings. The builder, the E.E. Paul Company, built the Stapleton, Tottenville, Port Richmond, Epiphany, Riverside, Muhlenberg Carnegie Branches for Carrere & Hastings, Architects, the Woodstock Branch for McKim, Mead & White, and the 58th Street Branch for Babb, Cook & Willard.

The entrance door and steps have been replaced. The windows have been replaced with windows having a similar fenestration pattern to the original. The basement windows have been closed up. The approximately 10,000 square foot interior has its original staircase with decorative iron rail. There is an oak paneled vestibule with marble wainscoting. There were rehabilitations in 1920 and 1956.

Notes: The library officially opened on February 19, 1906. The site cost $61,317 and the building and equipment $80,459, for a total of $141,776.

Current Information: This is the Muhlenberg Branch of The New York Public Library. Kliment & Halsband Architects will be developing plans for interior renovation and compliance with the Americans with Disabilities Act.

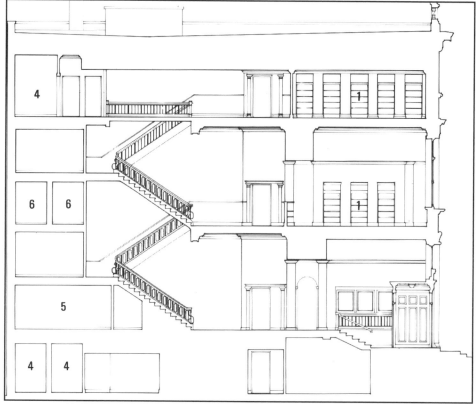

96th Street Branch Regional Library, 1993, Lisa Clifford, DGS Photographer;
Transverse Section, c. 1991 (Samuel J. De Santo and Associates).

96TH STREET BRANCH

Address   112-114 EAST 96TH STREET
Borough   MANHATTAN
Date   1905
Architects BABB, COOK & WILLARD

Description: The library is located on a busy two-way residential street with some ground floor storefronts. The 20th century apartment buildings vary from medium to high rise in height. The library is located in the middle of the block front and is built to the building line.

The three story limestone Renaissance Revival style building has tall, arched ground floor openings with scrolled keystones. The second floor windows are pedimented and a balustrade tops the modillioned cornice. The triangular pediment just above the door has a shield with an open book. There are bronze lanterns flanking the door. The library is similar to Babb, Cook & Willard's 67th Street Branch. The builder was Isaac Hopper & Son, who also worked with Babb, Cook & Willard on the St. Agnes Carnegie Branch, with McKim, Mead & White on the 115th Street Branch and with James Brown Lord on the Yorkville Branch.

On the outside the entrance door and the windows have been replaced, security grilles have been installed on the first floor windows, and the stone pillars at the steps have been removed. The over 13,000 square foot interior was renovated in 1991 by Samuel J. De Santo and Associates, architects. Original features include the high plaster ceilings, staircase with iron rail, rectangular plaster columns (but new capitals), and an oak paneled screen. Notable is the attention given to restoring the interior to a palette of colors sympathetic to the original period color scheme. There was also a major rehabilitation in 1960 by Bloch & Hesse architects.

Notes: The library officially opened on September 22, 1905. The site cost $33,030 and the building and equipment $79,297, for a total of $112,327.

Current Information: This is the 96th Street Regional Branch of The New York Public Library.

*115th Street Branch Library, 1993, Lisa Clifford, DGS Photographer; Interior, 1957
(Archives of The New York Public Library Astor, Lenox and Tilden Foundations).*

148

115TH STREET BRANCH

Address   203 WEST 115TH STREET
Borough   MANHATTAN
Date   1908
Architects McKIM, MEAD & WHITE

Description: The library is located in the middle of the block front on a residential street primarily lined with six story early 20th century tenements. There is a school across the street. The library is built to the building line.

The classical Renaissance Revival style building has a deeply rusticated stone facade. It is the only Carnegie with such bold rustication. The entrance is at the side bay on the front facade, the arched center window is marked by an elaborate cartouche with cupids on either side. The facade ends in a bracketed stone cornice. Lanterns, probably from a later date, flank the doorway. The builder was Isaac Hopper & Son, who also worked with McKim, Mead & White, Architects on the 115th Street Branch, with Babb, Cook & Willard, on the St. Agnes and 96th Street Carnegie Branches, with James Brown Lord on the Yorkville Branch.

On the exterior, the entrance door has been altered, a new rail has been added, the windows have been replaced, and the balustrade under the first floor windows has been filled in. The cornice was cut back in 1912 because it projected 10 inches beyond the property line. The over 12,000 square foot interior has an elegant vestibule with marble wainscoting, paneled ceiling, and a multi-paned screen on the side. The ceiling height is original but it is covered in acoustical tile. There are original round plaster columns, early or original wood paneling and display cases and the original staircase with decorative iron rail. Original pendant fixtures were replaced by modern fluorescent light fixtures. There was a rehabilitation in the 1953.

Notes: The library officially opened on November 6, 1908. The site cost $40,000 and the building and equipment $88,060, for a total of $128,060.

Current Information: This is the 115th Street Branch of The New York Public Library. It is a designated New York City Landmark and listed on the National and State Registers of Historic Places. Current plans include heating and ventilation upgrades, a new air conditioning system, and accessibility improvements.

125th Street Branch Library, 1993, Lisa Clifford, DGS Photographer;
Interior, c. 1910, Lewis Hine Photographer
(Archives of The New York Public Library Astor, Lenox and Tilden Foundations).

125TH STREET BRANCH

Address   224 EAST 125TH STREET
Borough   MANHATTAN
Date   1904
Architects McKIM, MEAD & WHITE

Description: The library is located in the middle of the block front on a wide busy commercial and residential street. It is surrounded by low and mid-rise 20th century masonry structures.

The handsome Renaissance Revival style building is three stories high and three bays wide. The entire limestone facade is rusticated, with arched windows and an entrance in one of the side bays on the front facade. The builder was Michael Reid & Company, who worked with McKim, Mead & White on all but two of their Carnegie branches. The McKim, Mead & White/Michael Reid Company Carnegie branches are: Chatham Square; 125th Street; 135th Street; Rivington; Kingsbridge; St. Gabriel's Park; Tompkins Square; Hamilton Grange; and Harlem.

On the exterior the entrance door and the windows have been replaced, the ground floor windows have been shortened, the large original lanterns at the doorway have been replaced by smaller, later lanterns. The over 13,000 square foot interior features a high, beamed plaster ceiling supported by typical round plaster columns with molded capitals and bases. There is a vestibule with paneled wood walls and a wooden screen with a transom. The original staircase and iron rail and the old book elevator have survived but modern fluorescent light fixtures replaced the original hanging incandescent lights. The library was rehabilitated in 1953-4.

Notes: The library officially opened on March 7, 1904. It was the third Carnegie branch of The New York Public Library to open. Lewis Cass Ledyard spoke for The New York Public Library. New York Times (3/8/1904, 9:5) The site cost $38,100 and the building and equipment $78,352, for a total of $116,452.

Current Information: This is the 125th Street Branch of The New York Public Library. When it opened, it was called the Harlem Branch, but the Carnegie at 9-11 West 124th Street assumed that name after it was opened in 1909 and is still known as the Harlem Branch today. Current projects include an auditorium rehabilitation, fence rehabilitation, accessibility improvements, and a rehabilitation of the heating and air conditioning systems.

Riverside Branch Library, Exterior, n.d., c. 1905; Interior, c. 1910, Lewis Hine Photographer
(Archives of The New York Public Library Astor, Lenox and Tilden Foundations).

RIVERSIDE BRANCH

Address   190-192 AMSTERDAM AVENUE
Borough   MANHATTAN
Date   1905
Architects CARRERE & HASTINGS

Description: The library was situated in a residential neighborhood near the corner of West 69th Street. The monumental stone Classical Revival style building was three stories high and four bays wide. There were three tall arched windows and an arched entrance on the ground floor. The upper floors were reminiscent of the Yorkville and Chatham Square libraries, with two-story Ionic columns separating the windows. The facade ended in a stone balustrade. The builder, the E.E. Paul Company, built the Stapleton, Tottenville, Port Richmond, Epiphany, Riverside, Muhlenberg Carnegie Branches for Carrere & Hastings, Architects, the Woodstock Branch for McKim, Mead & White, and the 58th Street Branch for Babb, Cook & Willard.

Notes: The library officially opened on February 16, 1905. The site cost $65,232 and the building and equipment $87,190, for a total of $152,422.

Current Information: The Riverside Branch of The New York Public Library was demolished and replaced by a new branch on the same site in 1965. That replacement branch was also recently decommissioned and the community is now served by a modern library facility across from the old site and near Lincoln Center.

Rivington Branch Library, 1993, Lisa Clifford, DGS Photographer;
Interior, c. 1910, Lewis Hine Photographer
(Archives of The New York Public Library Astor, Lenox and Tilden Foundations).

RIVINGTON BRANCH

Address   61-63 RIVINGTON STREET
Borough   MANHATTAN
Date   1905
Architects McKIM, MEAD & WHITE

Description: The library is located in the densely built Lower East Side, surrounded primarily by six story brick tenements dating from the early 20th century. The building is located in the middle of the block front and built to the building line.

The brick Classical Revival style building has a rusticated stone base. The three story, three bay library has two-story upper windows separated by brick pilaster with Corinthian capitals. The entrance door and the windows have been made significantly smaller than the original tall openings. The railing in front and the lanterns have been removed.

This library was the first to open a roof garden in the summer months. This open-air reading room was so popular that roof gardens were incorporated into the plans of four new branches: Hamilton Fish Park, William Seward Park, St. Gabriel's Park and Columbus. New York Times (4/24/1910, 9:4). The builder was Michael Reid & Company, who worked with McKim, Mead & White on all but two of their Carnegie branches. The McKim, Mead & White/Michael Reid Company Carnegie branches are: Chatham Square; 125th Street; 135th Street; Rivington; Kingsbridge; St. Gabriel's Park; Tompkins Square; Hamilton Grange; and Harlem.

Notes: The library officially opened on June 10, 1905. The site cost $45,500 and the building and equipment $77,399, for a total of $122,899.

Current Information: The Rivington Branch of The New York Public Library was decommissioned and is now occupied by the Chinese Nazarene Church.

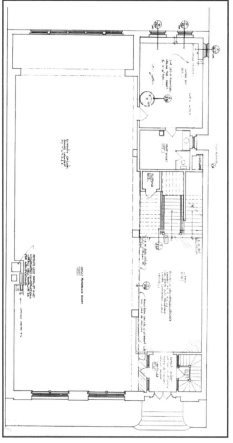

St. Agnes Branch Library, 1993,
Lisa Clifford, DGS Photographer;
1st Floor Renovation Plan, 1987,
Kirti Gandhi Consulting Engineer
(Department of General Services).

ST. AGNES BRANCH

Address   444-446 AMSTERDAM AVENUE
Borough   MANHATTAN
Date   1906
Architects BABB, COOK & WILLARD

Description: The library is located in the middle of the block front on busy Amsterdam Avenue in a bustling residential and commercial neighborhood. It lies within the Upper West Side Central Park West Historic District. Early 20th century four and five story brick tenements line the blocks. The library is built to the building line.

The three story, three bay Renaissance Revival style limestone library has an arched entrance in a side bay on the front facade. The facade ends in a stone balustrade above a modillioned cornice. The arched second floor windows have projecting pediments with ornamental stone carving. There are two bronze lanterns at the entrance. The builder was Isaac Hopper & Son, who also worked with Babb, Cook & Willard, Architects on the 96th Street Carnegie Branch, with McKim, Mead & White on the 115th Street Branch and with James Brown Lord on the Yorkville Branch.

On the outside, the entrance door and the windows have been replaced, the arches have been filled in, and the original iron fence has been partly removed. The almost 18,000 square foot interior has an oak paneled vestibule and oak paneled rectangular columns with molded capitals. There was a major rehabilitation in 1953. In 1995, pendant lights were reintroduced on the first and second floors.

Notes: The library officially opened on March 26, 1906. The site cost $65,000 and the building and equipment $97,027, for a total of $162,027. In 1949, the building custodian lived in a five room apartment in the building and was paid $3110 a year.

Current Information: This is the St. Agnes Branch of The New York Public Library. It is located within the New York City Upper West Side-Central Park West Historic District. The current projects include renovation of the community room by Sen Architects.

*St. Gabriel's Branch Library,
Exterior, n.d., c. 1908; Interior,
c. 1910, Lewis Hine Photographer
(Archives of The New York Public
Library Astor, Lenox and Tilden
Foundations).*

ST. GABRIEL'S PARK BRANCH

Address	303-5 EAST 36TH STREET
Borough	MANHATTAN
Date	1908
Architects	McKIM, MEAD & WHITE

Description: The library was located next to the corner of Second Avenue, in a residential neighborhood. The four story, three bay stone Renaissance Revival style building had an entrance in a side bay on the front facade. The stone facade was rusticated. There were arched openings at the first and second floors. The library had a fanciful fourth floor belvedere, enclosed by columns and a balustrade. The builder was Michael Reid & Company, who worked with McKim, Mead & White on all but two of their Carnegie branches. The McKim, Mead & White/Michael Reid Company Carnegie branches are: Chatham Square; 125th Street; 135th Street; Rivington; Kingsbridge; St. Gabriel's Park; Tompkins Square; Hamilton Grange; and Harlem.

Notes: The library officially opened on May 15, 1908. The site cost $48,000 and the building and equipment $91,209, for a total of $139,209.

Current Information: The St. Gabriel's Park Branch of The New York Public Library was decommissioned and is no longer standing. The site is now part of the approach to the Midtown Tunnel.

Schomburg Collection for Research in Black Culture, 1993, Lisa Clifford,
DGS Photographer; Interior, n.d., c. 1905
(Archives of The New York Public Library Astor, Lenox and Tilden Foundations).

SCHOMBURG COLLECTION FOR RESEARCH IN BLACK CULTURE

Address   103 WEST 135TH STREET
Borough   MANHATTAN
Date   1905
Architects McKIM, MEAD & WHITE

Description: The library is located in the middle of the block front on a busy two-way residential and commercial street. The nearby buildings are primarily six story early 20th century row houses, with modern high-rise housing projects across the street. There is a school across the street. The library is built to the building line in front but has open space on either side. The east side is now a garden connecting the old library to the new Schomburg buildings on Malcolm X Boulevard.

The Classical Revival style, three story, six bay stone library has a rusticated base with an entrance in a side bay on the front facade. There is a large central arched window with a decorative metal tympanum. The upper windows are separated by pilasters with decorative capitals. The flat roof ends in a deeply projecting cornice. The iron fence and granite steps are intact but the lanterns flanking the doorway have been removed. The builder was Michael Reid & Company, who worked with McKim, Mead & White on all but two of their Carnegie branches. The McKim, Mead & White/Michael Reid Company Carnegie branches are: Chatham Square; 125th Street; 135th Street; Rivington; Kingsbridge; St. Gabriel's Park; Tompkins Square; Hamilton Grange; and Harlem.

On the exterior the entrance door and the windows have been replaced and new windows have been added to the side facade. The more than 11,000 square foot interior has been recently completely renovated to provide office and gallery space for the buildings of the Schomburg Center. The original wood paneled vestibule, round plaster columns, and staircase with iron railing are the only original features.

Notes: The library officially opened as the 135th Street Branch on July 14, 1905. The site cost $28,000 and the building and equipment $75,282, for a total of $103,282. In the 1920's the Branch Librarian, Ernestine Rose, started a collection of African American literature which was very popular. In 1926 The New York Public Library purchased the Schomburg Collection of African American literature and art with a $10,000 gift from the Carnegie Corporation. Because of this collection, the Branch became a center of the Harlem Renaissance. In 1941 a large rear addition, the Countee Cullen Branch Library, was opened and the collection was moved there. In 1980 the Countee Cullen became the neighborhood branch library when a new building to house the collection, now called the Schomburg Center for Research in Black Culture. Another section was added between the new building and the Carnegie library in 1991.

Current Information: This Carnegie Branch, originally known as the 135th Street Branch, is now part of the Schomburg Center for Research in Black Culture of The New York Public Library, a complex of attached buildings. The Carnegie branch building is a designated New York City Landmark and is listed on the National and New York State Registers of Historic Places.

Seward Park Branch Library, 1993, Lisa Clifford, DGS Photographer;
Interior, c. 1910, Lewis Hine Photographer
(Archives of The New York Public Library Astor, Lenox and Tilden Foundations).

SEWARD PARK BRANCH

Address   192 EAST BROADWAY
Borough   MANHATTAN
Date   1909
Architects BABB, COOK & WELCH

Description: The library is located in a neighborhood with a wide variety of low to high-rise residential and institutional structures dating from the 19th and 20th century. The library is located at the eastern side of Seward Park.

The four story, three bay Renaissance Revival style stone building has an unusual plan, due to the irregularly-shaped site. Instead of the characteristic flat facade, the one bay wide entrance wing projects one full bay from the facade. A wrought iron fence encloses the space between the sidewalk and the facade. There is a rusticated stone base, corner quoins and bracketed pediments over the windows. The brick upper stories have large stone quoins. A roof garden, no longer in operation, was open in the warm weather and used as an outdoor reading room. The builder was Richard Deeves & Son, who also built the Morrisania Carnegie Branch for Babb, Cook & Willard, Architects and the West 40th Street Carnegie Branch for Cook & Welch.

The exterior door and windows have been replaced, although the windows have the same fenestration pattern as the originals. The spacious, over 20,000 square foot interior has a wood paneled vestibule, high plaster ceilings, rectangular plaster columns, and simple wood window trim. The original pendant fixtures were replaced by modern fluorescent lighting. There was a major rehabilitation in about 1953.

Notes: The library officially opened on November 11, 1909. The site cost $216,500 and the building and equipment $150,153, for a total of $366,653, making it the most expensive of the Carnegies. In choosing the site for the Seward Park Branch, the decision was made to build a large library centrally located and on a corner site rather than several small libraries.

Current Information: This is the Seward Park Branch of The New York Public Library.

67th Street Branch Library, Exterior, 1993, Lisa Clifford, DGS Photographer; Exterior, 1916
Interior, n.d. c. 1910(Archives of The New York Public Library Astor, Lenox and Tilden

67TH STREET BRANCH

Address   328 EAST 67TH STREET
Borough   MANHATTAN
Date   1905
Architects   BABB, COOK & WILLARD

Description: The library is located in the middle of the block front in a quiet residential neighborhood. There is a high school across the street. The architecture is varied, with late 19th and early 20th six story century tenements and later 20th century apartment and institutional buildings. The library is built to the building line.

The three story, three bay Renaissance Revival style limestone building has tall arched openings with scrolled keystones and an entrance in one of the two side bays on the front facade. There is an unusual Art Nouveau style transom above the arched doorway, which is flanked by lanterns. The second floor windows are rectangular with projecting pediments. The facade ends in a modillioned cornice. The builder was William L. Crow, who also built the Mott Haven Carnegie Branch for Babb, Cook & Willard, Architects and the Brooklyn Saratoga and Walt Whitman Carnegie Branches for Daus & Otto, Architects.

On the exterior, the entrance door and the windows have been replaced and the skylight has been removed. The basement window well has been partly filled in.   The over 14,000 square foot interior is entered by a graceful, curved wood paneled vestibule. There is a molded plaster ceiling supported by rectangular plaster columns with molded capitals and the original staircase with decorative iron railing. Modern fluorescent light fixtures have replaced the original incandescent hanging fixtures. The third floor is extant but no longer used. A new roof was installed and other work was done in 1939 and there was a major rehabilitation in 1952-3.

Notes: The library officially opened on January 20, 1905. The site cost $16,000 and the building and equipment $84,401, for a total of $100,401. When Ellen Auchmaty of Lenox, Massachusetts sold the land to the City for $16,000 she placed a stipulation in the deed that the character of the building be similar to the Yorkville Carnegie Branch. This library is almost identical to Babb, Cook & Willard's 96th Street Carnegie but shares general characteristics with the Yorkville Carnegie.

Current Information: This is the 67th Street Branch of The New York Public Library. Current projects include a Building Management System and improvements to comply with the Americans with Disabilities Act.

Tompkins Square Branch Library, Exterior, 1993, Lisa Clifford,
DGS Photographer; Interior, c. 1910, Lewis Hine Photographer
(Archives of The New York Public Library Astor, Lenox and Tilden Foundations).

TOMPKINS SQUARE BRANCH

Address   331 EAST 10TH STREET
Borough   MANHATTAN
Date   1904
Architects McKIM, MEAD & WHITE

Description: The library is located in the middle of the block front, in a residential neighborhood across from Tompkins Square Park. The block contains primarily five story 19th century masonry tenements and row houses. The immediate neighbors are five story tenements, some with ground floor stores. The library is built to the building line.

The elegant three story, three bay Classical Revival limestone building is more monumental than the surrounding buildings, with higher floor heights and larger door and windows. The ground floor has a tall arched doorway at one of the two side bays and two equally tall windows to the right. The arched second floor windows have decorative stone tympanums. The building is topped by an austere classical cornice with a decorative frieze. The builder was Michael Reid & Company, who worked with McKim, Mead & White, Architects on all but two of their Carnegie branches. The McKim, Mead & White/Michael Reid Company Carnegie branches are: Chatham Square; 125th Street; 135th Street; Rivington; Kingsbridge; St. Gabriel's Park; Tompkins Square; Hamilton Grange; and Harlem.

The windows and entrance door have been replaced. There was a major rehabilitation in 1960-1. At that time it was decided to keep the third floor rather than removing it.

Notes: The Tompkins Square Carnegie Branch officially opened on December 1, 1904. The site cost $50,000 and the building and equipment $85,028, for a total of $135,028.

Current Information: This is the Tompkins Square Branch of The New York Public Library. Current plans by RKT&B Architects call for major rehabilitation, including new exits from the restored third floor and handicapped accessibility improvements. Construction is scheduled for completion in 1996. This library is part of The New York Public Library's Adopt-a-Branch program.

Washington Heights Branch Library, 1993, Lisa Clifford, DGS Photographer;
Interior, 1956, Fred Stein Photographer
(Archives of The New York Public Library Astor, Lenox and Tilden Foundations).

WASHINGTON HEIGHTS BRANCH

Address   1000-1002 ST. NICHOLAS AVENUE
Borough   MANHATTAN
Date   1914
Architects CARRERE & HASTINGS

Description: The library is located on a busy, two way commercial and residential street. It is adjacent to Sylvan Terrace, a designated New York City landmark. The neighborhood architecture is primarily six story tenements and apartment buildings dating from the first half of the 20th century.

The three story, three bay red brick Georgian Revival style building has a granite base and a simple molded stone cornice. The arched doorway is at one of the side bays and there are arched windows at the second floor. Due to the hilly site, there are unusually high basement windows and small, high first floor windows. This atypical plan is reflected on the interior, where the formal entrance stairs lead both to the basement and the first floor. There are small lanterns flanking the door. This was the only Carnegie library project for the builder, Norcross Brothers & Company.

The entrance door and the windows have been replaced, although the fenestration pattern is similar to the original. The approximately 16,000 square foot interior is largely intact. Outstanding early or original features include the staircase with its decorative metal rail, the wood ornament and paneling of the vestibule, wall screens, and office partitions, the oak stacks, wooden book elevator, and the paneled oak charge desk.

Notes: The Washington Heights Branch officially opened on February 26th, 1914. The site cost $38,000 and the building and equipment $124,485, for a total of $162,485. The branch was a successor to the Washington Heights Free Library.

Current Information: This is the Washington Heights Branch of The New York Public Library. Current plans call for waterproofing the building and the installation of a Building Management System.

Webster Branch Library, 1993, Lisa Clifford, DGS Photographer; Interior, n.d., c. 1906, (Archives of The New York Public Library Astor, Lenox and Tilden Foundations).

WEBSTER BRANCH

Address   1465 YORK AVENUE
Borough   MANHATTAN
Date   1906
Architects BABB, COOK & WILLARD

Description: The library is located near the corner, in a residential and commercial neighborhood of structures which vary in height and date of construction. It sits on busy two way York Avenue across the street from P.S. 158.

The three story, three bay limestone Classical Revival style library has a tall arched doorway located in one of the two side bays and tall arched ground floor windows to the left. The date the cornerstone was laid, 1905, is carved on a rondel at the transom. The second floor windows have heavy arched pediments with shields under the arches. The bronze lanterns and stone pillars at the entrance have survived. The architecture firm, Babb, Cook & Willard, designed eight Carnegies. The builder was J.C. Vreeland & Company, which also built the St. George Branch on Staten Island for Carrere & Hastings, Architects.

The entrance door and the windows have been replaced but the fenestration pattern of the replacement windows is similar to the original. Security grilles have been added to the lower windows. The approximately 12,000 square foot interior has the original staircase with decorative metal rail, original plaster ceiling with cove molding, and wood paneled wall screen and charge desk. An early or original bulletin board has survived. In 1995, pendant lights replaced modern fixtures in an effort to introduce a more sympathetic lighting design for this Carnegie branch.

Notes: The Webster Branch officially opened on October 24th, 1906. The site cost $15,000 and the building and equipment $73,763 for a total of $88,763.

Current Information: This is the Webster Branch of The New York Public Library. Current plans call for upgrading the heating, ventilation and air conditioning system, and a Building Management system to control all operational systems within the building.

West 40th Street Branch Library, 1995, Lisa Clifford, DGS Photographer; Exterior, 1904, Wurts Brothers Photographers (Archives of The New York Public Library Astor, Lenox and Tilden Foundations).

WEST 40TH STREET BRANCH

Address 457 WEST 40TH STREET
Borough MANHATTAN
Date 1913
Architects COOK & WELCH

Description: The library is located in the middle of the block front in an industrial area across from a Lincoln Tunnel access ramp. It is built to the building line. Originally this library was in a residential neighborhood composed primarily of late 19th and early 20th century tenements.

The three story, three bay limestone library has an arched entrance, which no longer functions as an entrance. The rusticated ground floor sits over a high granite base. The arched second floor windows and rectangular third floor windows are highlighted by simple molding. The entrance door and the windows have been extensively altered. The builder was Richard Deeves & Company, who also built the Morrisania Carnegie Branch for Babb, Cook & Willard, Architects and the Seward Park Carnegie for Cook & Welch.

Notes: The library officially opened on October 20, 1913. The site cost $28,000 and the building and equipment $119,012, for a total of $147,012.

Current Information: The West 40th Street Branch of The New York Public Library was decommissioned and is now part of the Covenant House complex.

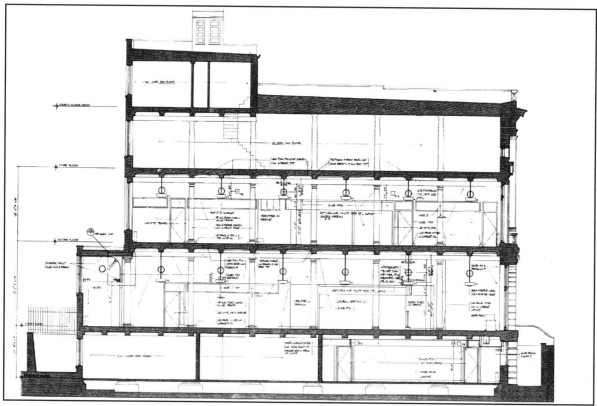

Yorkville Branch Library, 1993, Lisa Clifford, DGS Photographer; Longitudinal Section, 1985, Gwathmey Siegel and Associates Architects (Department of General Services).

YORKVILLE BRANCH

Address   222 EAST 79TH STREET
Borough   MANHATTAN
Date   1902
Architect JAMES BROWN LORD

Description: The library is located in the middle of the block front in a residential neighborhood on a busy two-way cross street. The neighborhood architecture consists primarily of 15 to 20 story high, 20th century apartment buildings mixed in with four story 19th century row houses. The library is built to the building line.

The three story, three bay Beaux Arts style Indiana limestone building has an arched entrance in one of the two side bays on the front facade. The ground floor is rusticated; the two upper floors are set back behind massive Ionic columns and a stone balustrade. The stone carving is more elaborate than that of the other Carnegies, with lion's head keystones on the ground floor and swags and garlands with heads in the center on the third floor. A fourth story, not visible from the street, held a custodian's apartment. The stone cornice had to be shaved at both sides because it hung over onto the adjacent properties. The builder was Isaac Hopper & Son, who also built the St. Agnes, 96th Street and 115th Street Carnegie Branches.

The over 13,000 square foot interior was recently renovated. The original staircase with its decorative iron rail has been retained but enclosed, the high plaster ceiling and round plaster columns with molded capitals have survived. On the exterior the entrance door and the windows have been replaced, although the decorative transoms are intact.

Notes: The library was officially opened on December 13th, 1902. It was the first Carnegie library to be built in New York City. This library was planned before the Carnegie bequest and was selected to be the first Carnegie-funded branch. There was a previous Yorkville branch in a storefront at 1523 Second Avenue. The architects' committee had not yet been formed when James Brown Lord was selected as architect. He died the year the library was opened. The plan of this branch conformed with the plans agreed upon by the newly formed Advisory Board of Architects. The design of the library influenced the later Carnegie branches and a reflection of the facade can be seen on McKim, Mead & White's Chatham Square Branch, which opened a year later.

Dr. John S. Billings, Director of The New York Public Library, spoke at the ceremonies and conveyed the regrets of Andrew Carnegie, who was unable to attend. Lewis Cass Ledyard, Trustee of The New York Public Library spoke as did Arthur E. Bostwick, who noted in his speech that there were 14 libraries under the aegis of The New York Public Library. New York Times (12/14/1902, 7:5) The site cost $30,000 and the building and equipment $71,979 for a total of 101,979.

Current Information: This is the Yorkville Branch of The New York Public Library. The building is a designated New York City Landmark and listed on the National and State Registers of Historic Places. The branch has recently undergone extensive interior renovation.

INVENTORY OF
CARNEGIE LIBRARIES
OF NEW YORK CITY

THE NEW YORK PUBLIC LIBRARY

STATEN ISLAND

St. George /CRW ★

West New Brighton ●

Port Richmond ★

Stapleton ★

● Todt Hill-Westerleigh

South Beach ●

Dongan Hills ●

● New Dorp

Great Kills ●

Huguenot Park ●

Tottenville ★

The New York Public Library 1996

★ *Operating Carnegie Libraries*

☆ *Former Carnegie Libraries or sites*

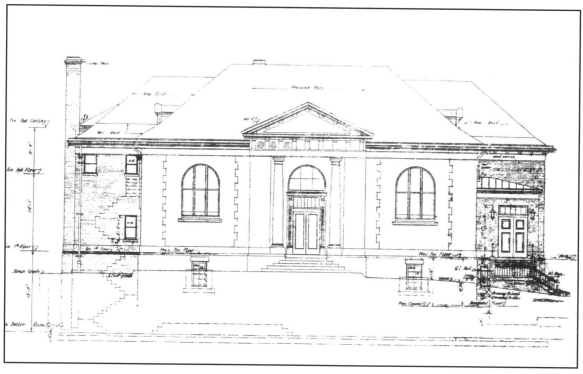

Port Richmond Branch Library, Exterior, 1993, Lisa Clifford, DGS Photographer;
Elevation of 1932 Alteration and Addition (Department of General Services).

PORT RICHMOND BRANCH

Address   75 BENNETT STREET
Borough   STATEN ISLAND
Date   1905
Architects   CARRERE & HASTINGS

Description: The library is located on a corner site, set back on a plot of land. The one story, three bay Classical Revival style red brick building has stone trim. The projecting center entrance has a full pediment with a decorative frieze. Tall columns flank the entrance. The arched windows are set in a wide block of stone trim. There are deeply overhanging eaves. The library is very similar to Carrere & Hastings' Stapleton Carnegie Branch. The builder, the E.E. Paul Company, built the Stapleton, Tottenville, Port Richmond, Epiphany, Riverside, Muhlenberg Carnegie Branches for Carrere & Hastings, Architects, the Woodstock Branch for McKim, Mead & White, and the 58th Street Branch for Babb, Cook & Willard. There were major alterations and an addition in 1938-9 with WPA funds. These included the lower level auditorium. The original wood shingled roof was replaced in 1967.

Notes: The library officially opened on March 18, 1905. The site cost $5,000 and the building and equipment $25,398, for a total of $30,398.

Current Information: This is the Port Richmond Branch of The New York Public Library. Current plans call for renovation of the basement auditorium, including upgrading the finishes, lighting, audiovisual system and stage equipment and the installation of a Building Management System.

St. George Branch Borough Library Center, Exterior, 1993, Lisa Clifford, DGS Photographer;
Construction Completion Photograph of 1952 Addition (Department of General Services).

ST. GEORGE BRANCH

Address 450 ST. MARKS PLACE
Borough STATEN ISLAND
Date 1907
Architects CARRERE & HASTINGS

Description: The library sits on a prominent site, on a ridge, and surrounded by three streets. There is a large lawn at the rear. The building is in the Staten Island Civic Center, next to the Borough Hall and next to the St. George commercial district. A large handicapped access ramp is located on the side of the building.

The two and one half story, nine bay red brick Classical Revival style building has stone trim and a stone base. There are small dormers on the hipped roof. The pedimented center entrance is flanked by two arched windows. The builder was the J. C. Vreeland Building Company, who also built the Webster Carnegie Branch in Manhattan for Babb, Cook & Willard, Architects. There have been several major alterations to this building, most notably an enlargement in 1952 and renovations in 1963 and 1986. As part of the 1986 renovation the ceiling on the first floor was opened up to reveal the wooden beams and the arched rear windows were rebuilt to emphasize views of New York Harbor.

Notes: The library officially opened on June 26, 1907. The site cost $32,844 and the building and equipment $72,018, for a total of $104,862. The large library was built to be the main circulation library for Staten Island. It held administrative offices and a reference library. The architect, John Carrere, planned to make the building visually prominent and to have a clear view of the bay from the inside.

Current Information: This is the St. George Borough Library Center of The New York Public Library. There was a major renovation and addition by Helpern Architects in 1986. The David Wilson stained glass windows installed as part of the work won an Art Commission Award for Design Excellence. A current project includes elevator rehabilitation.

Stapleton Branch Library, Exterior 1993, Lisa Clifford, DGS Photographer, Interior, n.d., c. 1910 (Archives of The New York Public Library Astor, Lenox and Tilden Foundations).

STAPLETON BRANCH

Address   132 CANAL STREET
Borough   STATEN ISLAND
Date   1907
Architects CARRERE & HASTINGS

Description: The library is located on a corner site, surrounded by a plot of land. It is located across the street from Tappen Park, the center of the Village and the site of the Edgewater Village Hall, a designated New York City landmark.

The one story building is very similar to Carrere & Hastings' Port Richmond Carnegie Branch. The red brick and stone Classical Revival building is one story high and three bays wide, with a projecting pedimented center entrance. The flanking arched windows have wide stone trim. There are deeply overhanging bracketed eaves. The builder, the E.E. Paul Company, built the Stapleton, Tottenville, Port Richmond, Epiphany, Riverside, Muhlenberg Carnegie Branches for Carrere & Hastings, Architects, the Woodstock Branch for McKim, Mead & White, and the 58th Street Branch for Babb, Cook & Willard. The originally wood shingled roof was replaced in 1967. There were rehabilitations in 1939 and 1953.

Notes: The library officially opened on June 17, 1907. The site cost $16,558 and the building and equipment $40,191, for a total of $56,749.

Current Information: This is the Stapleton Branch of The New York Public Library. An extensive renovation is being designed by Ehrenkrantz & Eckstut Architects for exterior and interior modifications to accommodate the disabled, the renovation of the auditorium, the correction of water infiltration, roof replacement, and the addition of a Building Maintenance System.

Tottenville Branch Library, Exterior and Interior, 1993, Lisa Clifford, DGS Photographer.

TOTTENVILLE BRANCH

Address   7430 AMBOY ROAD
Borough   STATEN ISLAND
Date   1904
Architects CARRERE & HASTINGS

Description: This branch library is set far back on a large plot of land. The land slopes sharply at the rear and affords wide vistas from the rear windows. The building is located in a suburban residential neighborhood in the southeastern corner of Staten Island. Three schools, including P.S. 1 and I.S. 34, are nearby.

It is similar to the Port Richmond and Stapleton Carnegie Branches, also by Carrere & Hastings, but is larger than the other two. The one story, five bay Classical revival style building has stone trim. The projecting center entrance has a full pediment, with columns flanking the entrance. The arched windows are set in wide frames of stone. There is a hipped roof with overhanging eaves. The builder, the E.E. Paul Company, built the Stapleton, Tottenville, Port Richmond, Epiphany, Riverside, Muhlenberg Carnegie Branches for Carrere & Hastings, Architects, the Woodstock Branch for McKim, Mead & White, and the 58th Street Branch for Babb, Cook & Willard.

On the exterior, the entrance door and the windows have been replaced. On the interior, there is a restored high beamed ceiling, pedimented trim at the entrance door and simple wood trim on the windows. Some of the original millwork was replaced in renovations of the interior.

Notes: The library officially opened on November 26, 1904. The site cost $601 and the building and equipment $27,170, for a total of $27,771. It was the first Carnegie branch on Staten Island and the first branch of the New York Public Library in that borough. Before the Carnegie branch was built, the Tottenville community was served by the library opened in 1899 in a two-room house by the Philemon Library and Historical Society.

Current Information: This is the Tottenville Branch of The New York Public Library. A major exterior restoration and interior renovation designed by John Ellis/Stephen D. Weinstein, Joint Venture Architects, was completed in 1993. The design for handicapped access to the building won an Art Commission Award for Design Excellence in 1991. Upon completion of construction, the project won the Municipal Art Society fifth annual New York Preservation Award and a Preservation League of Staten Island Award.

INVENTORY OF CARNEGIE LIBRARIES OF NEW YORK CITY

THE QUEENS BOROUGH PUBLIC LIBRARY

QUEENS

Steinway

Whitestone

★ **Poppenhusen**

Bay Terrace

★ **Astoria**

Mitchell-Linden

Ravenswood

East Elmhurst

Auburndale-Clearview

Douglaston
Little Neck

Queensbridge

Broadway

Langston Hughes

McGoldrick

Court Square

Jackson Heights

☆ Flushing

East Flushing

Bayside

North Hills

Woodside

Corona

Queensboro Hill

Sunnyside

Elmhurst ★

Windsor Park

Glen Oaks

Lefrak City

Fresh Meadows

Maspeth

Rego Park

Pomonok

Hillcrest

Bellerose

Forest Hills

Vleigh

Queens Village

Middle Village

Hollis

North Forest Park

Briarwood

Central
Library

South Hollis

Ridgewood

Glendale

Richmond Hill ★

St. Albans

★ **Woodhaven**

South Jamaica

Lefferts

Cambria Heights

Ozone Park

Baisley Park

South Ozone Park

Rochdale Village

Laurelton

Howard Beach

Rosedale

Broad
Channel

Peninsula

Arverne

Far Rockaway ☆

Seaside

The Queens Borough
Public Library 1996

★ *Operating Carnegie Libraries*

☆ *Former Carnegie Libraries or sites*

Astoria Branch Library, Exterior, 1993, Lisa Clifford, DGS Photographer;
Exterior, n.d., c. 1904 (Queens Library: Long Island Collection)

ASTORIA BRANCH

Address   14-01 ASTORIA BOULEVARD
Borough   QUEENS
Date   1904
Architects TUTHILL & HIGGINS

Description: The Astoria branch library is located on busy, commercial Astoria Boulevard. The neighborhood contains a mix of one to three story primarily brick residential, commercial and industrial buildings, built mainly in the twentieth century. There is a nineteenth century cemetery in back of the building. Although the population in the community has declined, the Astoria branch still provides an anchor for the neighborhood. The library sits on a corner lot, surrounded by a simple wrought iron fence with decorative iron posts. There was originally a low brick retaining wall around the site. At the rear there is a curved brick bench which matches the brick of the building. This bench must have been provided for library users, extending the library services to the outside.

The orange brick building stands one story high over a high basement. There is stone trim around the windows and at the base. The building originally had an angled corner entrance topped by a Flemish Revival style curved gable, unlike any of the other Queens Carnegies. This entrance was squared off, creating two new windows and a new entrance, possibly in the 1930's when there were renovations to the building by the Federal Civil Works Administration, a Depression Era work relief project. The basement windows were made wider at this time and a children's entrance was added on the side at the basement level. The brick used matched the original very closely and the window decoration is identical. The roof, originally tile, was altered and covered with slate probably at this time. At a later date, possibly in the late 1960's, a new red brick entrance bay and staircase were built. The lower half of three of the large, tri-partite windows was bricked in with the same red brick and new aluminum windows were installed.

Inside, there is a modern, open library space with little or no evidence of the original details. The original interior had a domed ceiling, ornamental columns and hardwood floors. The two WPA murals in the basement were part of a group of five painted for the Children's Reading Room by Max Spivak (1906-1981). The brightly colored murals depicting puppets and the sculptures of circus performers, were originally a collaboration. Three of the murals and all of the sculptures are now lost. There were renovations in the 1930's, the 1960's and again in 1989, when a new circulation desk was installed and exterior windows were replaced.

Notes: The library opened on November 19, 1904 with a ceremony and speeches by the president of The Queens Borough Library, Dr. Walter Frey, the NYC Corporation Counsel, John Delany, and the director of The New York Public Library, Dr. John Billings. The total cost of the library, including equipment, was $47,208: $11,000 for the site and $36,208 for the building and equipment. An Astoria branch library was in existence for five years before the Carnegie building opened.

Current Information: This is the Astoria Branch of The Queens Borough Public Library. Current plans include replacement of the air conditioning cooling tower and the boiler.

Elmhurst Branch Library, Exterior, 1993, Lisa Clifford, DGS Photographer.

ELMHURST BRANCH

Address   86-01 BROADWAY
Borough   QUEENS
Date   1906
Architects LORD & HEWLETT

Description: The Elmhurst branch library is located in the heart of Elmhurst, a busy commercial area with a mix of nineteenth and twentieth century residential and commercial frame and masonry structures. The building sits on a triangle lot, enclosed by a simple wrought iron fence similar but not identical to the fences of the other Queens Carnegie libraries. The landscape around the library is a community garden today, with volunteers maintaining the planting. An original landscaped garden at the rear with rustic furniture which is now a parking lot. At Elmhurst as well at Richmond Hill, Woodhaven and Flushing, there were tall, cone shaped conifers evenly spaced about one bay apart directly in front of the building, that are now gone.

The Georgian Revival classical library is a one story, five bay orange-colored brick building with a central entrance. The large metal cornice below the parapet is not original. According to early photographs, there was a stone balustrade above an imposing modillioned cornice. There are brick lintels and stone sills on the rectangular, tri-partite windows. The entrance is marked by a molded pediment. This library is similar to the Flushing branch (now demolished); the builders were H. F. Quinn & Sons.

The library has been renovated several times and the original windows and entrance doors have been replaced with modern aluminum variations or bricked in. A modern handicapped access ramp and concrete steps with an aluminum pipe rail have been installed at the entrance. A rear children's room wing appears to have been added. There were renovations in the 1930's, with some work being done by the Federal Civil Works Administration, a Depression work relief project and in 1961, when new windows, roof, mechanical systems were installed and the interior was renovated. Alterations in 1980 left intact the original plaster ceiling and the Colonial Revival style wooden mantel decorated the library seal in the Children's Room. In 1985 a new circulation desk and lighted display shelves were installed and an adult learning center was constructed.

Notes: There was controversy over the selection of the site, a characteristics occurence with Carnegie branches. There were offers to donate land for a library site by several people, including a real estate developer but the Library Board had already picked a prominent site on Broadway. There were angry public meetings but the Library Board prevailed and the building was constructed on Broadway. The library was opened on March 31, 1906 with presentations by Philip Frank sand by Walter Bogert, both members of the Queens Carnegie Committee and Joseph Bermel, Queens Borough President. The final cost was $46,246; $10,000 for the site and $32,246 for the building and equipment.

Current Information: This is the Elmhurst Branch of The Queens Borough Public Library. The library is slated for window and door replacements this year.

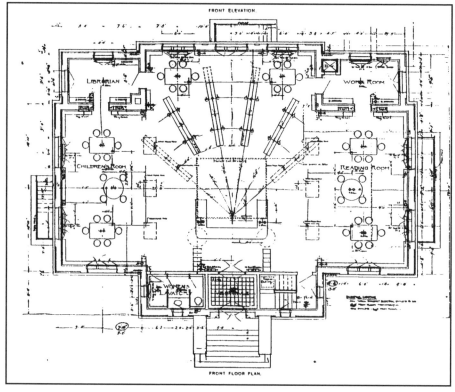

*Far Rockaway Branch Library, Exterior n.d., c. 1904,
(Queens Library: Long Island Collection);
First Floor Plan, The Brickbuilder, April 1905, v. 14.)*

FAR ROCKAWAY BRANCH

Address   1637 CENTRAL AVENUE
Borough   QUEENS
Date   1904
Architects LORD & HEWLETT

Description: The Far Rockaway branch library is no longer standing.   It was a one story, five bay brick building in an austere Classical Revival style. A flight of steps led to the door in the projecting center entrance bay.   The rectangular door and windows had keystone arches and the facade was topped by a molded stone cornice.   Located on a corner lot, it was surrounded by a simple lawn.   The builder was Richard Carman.

Notes: The site originally held an old schoolhouse owned by the Town of Hempstead and deeded to the Village of Far Rockaway.   Half of the land was used by the library, the rest was assigned to the Fire Department and the Municipal Court, whose building was already there.   The library opened on August 18, 1904 with presentations by Dr. Walter Frey, president of The Queens Borough Library and by Walter Bogert, both members of the Queens Carnegie Committee, and by John Delany, New York City Corporation Counsel.   The total cost of the library was $38,552, with the apportioned value of the site at $9,000 and the building and equipment costing $29,552. In the last decades, library use has declined but today the current replacement branch serves a growing immigrant population.

Current Information: The Carnegie library burned down in 1966 and was replaced by a new branch library on the same site.

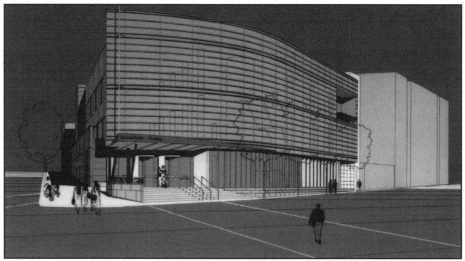

Flushing Branch Library, Exterior, n.d., c. 1906,
(Queens Library Long Island Collection); Elevation of New Flushing Branch, 1995
(James Stewart Polshek and Partners).

FLUSHING BRANCH

Address   41-25 MAIN STREET
Borough   QUEENS
Date   1906
Architects LORD & HEWLETT

Description: The Flushing branch library is no longer standing. It was a one story Georgian Revival style library very similar to the Elmhurst branch, also designed by Lord & Hewlett. The five bay brick building had a central entrance with pilasters separating the tall arched door and windows. There was a stone balustrade at the roof and enclosing a terrace in front of the building. Set on a corner lot, it was surrounded by a lawn. There were tapering conifers planted at the front facade soon after the building was built here as well as at Elmhurst.   A fence and shrubbery was added at an apparently early period.   The builder, Thomas Williams, also built the Poppenhusen Carnegie branch.

Notes: The building was opened on December 17, 1906. The total cost was $49,980. The site was partly donated - the rest cost 19,000, and the building and equipment cost $37,980. The Carnegie building replaced a library located in a small frame building on the same site.   The interior was described as looking more "like a beautiful drawing room than a public library." (*Thrift Broadcaster*, April, 1929, QBPL Collection)

The Flushing Library Association was established in 1858, with 800 books and 168 members. The subscription library was open only to members throughout most of the nineteenth century.   In 1902 the Flushing Library Association was consolidated with the Queens Borough Library.

Current Information: This Carnegie library was demolished in the mid-1950's and replaced by another branch library in 1957. The branch serves as the regional library for the northeastern quadrant of Queens. It serves a densely populated area with a large immigrant population and is second only to the Central Library in Jamaica in circulation and activity.   A new larger library has been designed for the site by James Stewart Polshek & Associates. Construction will begin in July, 1996.

Poppenhusen Branch Library, Exterior, 1993, Lisa Clifford, DGS Photographer;
Exterior, n.d., c. 1904 (Queens Library; Long Island Collection)

POPPENHUSEN BRANCH

Address 121-23 14TH AVENUE
Borough QUEENS
Date 1904
Architects HEINS & LAFARGE

Description: The library is located on a corner lot and surrounded by a lawn. There is a low stone wall marking the boundaries of the property. It is an integral part of the somewhat isolated College Point community and its use is expected to increase. There were over 70,000 users in 1993.

The exuberant Classical Revival style brick library is one story high with an unusual hipped roof. The five bay building has a slightly projecting pedimented entrance marked by a stone arch and horizontal stone banding. The builder was Thomas Williams, who built the demolished Flushing Carnegie branch for Lord & Hewlett architects. The original T-shaped building was expanded into a rectangle in the 1930s. There was a major renovation in 1963-4. In 1989 the entrance door and the windows were replaced.

Notes: The library opened on October 5, 1904 in a ceremony with presentations by Philip Frank, chairman of the Queens Carnegie Committee, the Queens Borough President Joseph Cassidy, the New York City Corporation Counsel, John Delany, and Arthur Bostwick of The New York Public Library. The site was donated by the local community and the total cost of the building and site was $30,114. The Poppenhusen Institute library provided the circulating library for the new building. The Poppenhusen Institute was a major local public library from 1870 until the Carnegie was opened in 1904.

Current Information: This is the Poppenhusen branch of The Queens Borough Public Library. There are current plans for exterior and interior renovations, including replacement/upgrade of the heating, ventilation and air conditioning systems, re-roofing of the two terraced wings, new flooring, ceilings, lighting, re-organization of the major interior spaces, and alterations for handicapped accessibility.

Richmond Hill Branch Library, Exterior, 1993, Lisa Clifford, DGS Photographer;
Interior, n.d., c. 1905 (Queens Library: Long Island Collection)

RICHMOND HILL BRANCH

Address 118-14 HILLSIDE AVENUE
Borough QUEENS
Date 1905
Architects TUTHILL & HIGGINS

Description: The library is situated on a large lot bounded by major thoroughfares and elevated railroad tracks. It is on the edge of a busy commercial area, surrounded by residential neighborhoods. The architecture is mixed, mostly twentieth century brick structures from one to six stories high. The library stands out because of its prominent location and extensive grounds. It is a focal point for the community and is the site for community holiday events and celebrations. The lot is surrounded by a wrought iron fence and a decorative brick fence. According to early photographs, there was no fencing immediately after it was built and there was a simple lawn in front. In 1908 the librarian H.M. Easby wrote that three visiting librarians from one of the Brooklyn branches asked why there were no plants and seats on the lawn in front of the building, confirming the original simple landscape. (March, 1908 Branch Report, QBPL Collection).

The library was enlarged and the grounds were laid out with more elaborate plantings, probably about two decades later. (A 1941 newspaper article in the QBPL Collection states that a large addition was made in 1929.) Today there are flagstone paths and the grounds are planted with flower borders at the fence with a lawn forming the rest of the landscape. There are modern steps and a handicapped access ramp with aluminum railings were added recently.

The austere Classical Revival style one story library was originally three bays wide with a projecting center entrance bay. The entrance is marked by flanking Ionic columns. Another bay was added, possibly in 1929, using the same dark tan brick and ornamental details. There is a dentilled cornice and a mansard roof, originally tiled with cresting, now gone. The exterior windows and doors have been replaced with modern aluminum versions. There is a standing seam metal roof which was installed in the 1960's.

The interior has been renovated several times. A new circulation desk and lighted display shelves were installed in 1985. An early photograph shows wooden wall shelves with paintings hung above, and wooden tables with bentwood chairs. Today there is a lowered ceiling, asphalt tile floors and very little of the original interior remains. There is a probably later than original Colonial Revival style mantel with the Queens Borough Public Library seal in the children's room. Column details and the mezzanine over the wooden stacks are surviving original features. There is a 160 square foot, 1936 WPA mural by Philip Evergood. The vividly colored mural depicts "The Story of Richmond Hill." Critically acclaimed at the time, it is a respected feature of the library today.

Notes: The library was opened on July 1, 1905 at a ceremony with a presentation by Dr. Walter Frey, president of The Queens Borough Library but listed on the opening program as Chairman of the Carnegie Committee. The New York City Corporation Counsel, John Delany, received the building. George Bissell, president of the Twentieth Century Club, gave an address. The total cost was $44,659, with the site at $12,000 and the building and equipment at $32,659. Richmond Hill had a circulating library in Arcanum Hall on Jamaica Avenue from 1898. It was founded by the Twentieth Century Club.

Current Information: This is the Richmond Hill Branch of The Queens Borough Public Library.

Woodhaven Branch Library, 1993, Lisa Clifford, DGS Photographer; Exterior, n.d., c. 1924 (Queens Library: Long Island Collection).

WOODHAVEN BRANCH

Address 85-41 FOREST PARKWAY
Borough QUEENS
Date 1924
Architect ROBERT F. SCHIRMER

Description: The Woodhaven branch is located in a quiet residential neighborhood of frame houses and brick apartment buildings dating from just after 1900, when Forest Parkway was opened. The building is situated on a corner lot and surrounded by a simple wrought iron fence. There is a lawn surrounding the building, primarily in front, with shrubbery planted near the facade. The library continues to be in the middle rank of circulation in the system, with over 61,000 users in 1993.

The austere Georgian Revival library is a five bay, one story brick building with cast stone trim. There are tall arched windows and a central door reminiscent of the demolished Flushing branch library. The architect was Robert F. Schirmer who, along with J. W. Schmidt, designed the 1927 central building of the Queens Borough Public Library, now the Queens Family Courthouse. The builders of the Woodhaven Branch were Fraser & Berau from Brooklyn.

There have been alterations over the years. The windows originally had multi-paned sash with fan light transoms. They have been reduced in size, with top arches and the lower third bricked-in and aluminum windows installed. The entrance doorway has also been bricked in on top and the door replaced with a modern aluminum and glass door. Modern concrete steps and a handicapped access ramp with an aluminum railing were installed in 1991.

A children's room and auditorium were added under the Federal Civil Works Administration work relief program in the early 1930's. The library was extensively renovated in the late 1960's, with a new roof, new windows, heating, ventilation and air conditioning systems. A fire in 1978 led to further work.

Notes: There was a library in Woodhaven in 1911, called the Manor branch and located on Jamaica Avenue. The Carnegie Library was opened on January 5, 1924. It was the last one built in Queens and was partially financed with the remaining money in the Carnegie gift.

Current Information: This is the Woodhaven Branch of The Queens Borough Public Library.

APPENDIX

SELECTED BIBILIOGRAPHY

American Architect and Building News. "Public Libraries of New York," v. 87, #1529, April 15, 1905, p. 123.

Architectural Record. "The Work of Carrere & Hastings," v. 27, January, 1910, p. 1-120.

Bobinski, George. *Carnegie Libraries: Their History and Impact on American Public Library Development.* Chicago: American Library Association, 1969.

_____. *Carnegie Libraries: Their Current and Future Status —The Results of a Survey.* Buffalo, New York, 1991.

Brickbuilder, The: v. 14, #4, #5; #7, April; May; July, 1905, Plates 31; 39; 55.

Brooklyn Public Library. *Scrapbooks.* 1902-1907; 1950-1957. (Contain newspaper clippings on BPL and branches.)

_____. *Branch Library Files.* 1901-c. 1960; c. 1950-1994. (Contain correspondence from Andrew Carnegie and Carnegie Committee, minutes of meetings, architects' and contractors' correspondence and contracts, financial data, site selection reports and correspondence, opening ceremony pamphlets, and miscellaneous related reports and pamphlets.)

_____. *Photograph Collection.* (Contains historic photographs of Carnegie Branches, by branch.)

Carnegie Committee. *Instructions to Architects.* Brooklyn, 1902, in Brooklyn Public Library Branch Library Files.

Dain, Phyllis. *The New York Public Library: A History of Its Founding Years.* New York: The New York Public Library, 1973.

Freeman, Margaret B., *The Brooklyn Public Library: A History.* New York, 1966.

Koch, Theodore Wesley. *A Portfolio of Carnegie Libraries.* Ann Arbor, Michigan: George Wahr, Publisher, 1907.

Koch, Theodore Wesley. *A Book of Carnegie Libraries.* New York City: The H.W. Wilson Company, 1917.

Lydenburg, Harry Miller. *History of the New York Public Library.* New York, 1923.

Marks, L.B. "Design of the Illumination of the New York City Carnegie Libraries," in *Transactions of the Illuminating Engineering Society,* a paper presented to the society in Philadelphia, October, 1908, paper located in The NYPL Archives..

New York City Department of Finance. *Real Estate Owned by the City of New York Under the Jurisdiction of the Presidents of the Boroughs.* New York, 1908.

New York City Department of Finance. *Record of Real Estate Owned by the City of New York.* New York, 1914.

New York City Department of General Services. *Plans and Drawings of Carnegie Branch*

Libraries. Selected Drawings of Carnegie Libraries from the DGS Archives.

New York Times. Selected Articles on Andrew Carnegie and Carnegie Libraries, 1900-1920.

Rub, Timothy. "The Day of Big Operations: Andrew Carnegie and his Libraries," *Architectural Record* (July, 1985) 81-85.

Sink, Robert. "Democratic Images, Children in the Library: Lewis Hine's Photographs for the Child Welfare Exhibit of 1911," *Biblion*: V.1, #2, Spring, 1993.

Sturgis, Russell. "The Carnegie Libraries in New York City, *Architectural Record* v. 17, March, 1905."

The New York Public Library. *Agreement Entered into with the City of New York Relative to the Gift of Andrew Carnegie for Branch Free Circulating Library Buildings.* New York, July 17, 1901, in The NYPL Archives.

The New York Public Library Archives. *Record Groups 5, 6, 8, and 10.* (Extensive files of correspondence, contracts, specifications, memoranda, reports, and historic photographs relating to the Carnegie branch libraries.)

The Queens Borough Public Library. *Branch Library Files.* 1901-c. 1960. (Contain brochures, booklets, reports of Branch librarians, contracts, correspondence, postcards, and other miscellaneous reports and documents.)

_____. *Branch Library Scrapbooks.* 1901-c. 1960. (Contain newspaper clippings, correspondence, library information sheets and pamphlets.)

_____. *Historic Photograph Collection* (Contains historic photographs of Carnegie branches.)

_____. *The Queens Borough Public Library Project.* New York: QBPL, 1934.

Toan, Danforth. "Libraries," *Encyclopedia of Architecture: Design, Engineering & Construction.* V. 3, New York: John Wiley & Sons, 1989, 220-268.

Van Slyck, Abigail A. "The Utmost Amount of Effectiv [sic] Accommodation: Andrew Carnegie and the Reform of the American Library," *Journal of the Society of Architectural Historians,* L (December, 1991) 359-383.

Von Skal, George. *Illustrated History of the Borough of Queens.* New York, 1908.

Wall, Joseph Frazier. *Andrew Carnegie.* Pittsburgh: University of Pittsburgh Press, 1989.

ORIGINAL ARCHITECTS

RAYMOND ALMIRALL
Bushwick, BPL (1908)
Eastern Parkway, BPL (1914)
Pacific, BPL (1903)
Park Slope, BPL (1906)

BABB, COOK & WELCH
Seward Park, NYPL (1909)

BABB, COOK & WILLARD
Columbus, NYPL (1909)
58th Street, NYPL (1907)
Mirrisania, NYPL (1908)
Mott Haven, NYPL (1905)
96th Street, NYPL (1905)
St. Agnes, NYPL (1908)
67th Street, NYPL (1905)
Webster, NYPL (1906)

CARRERE & HASTINGS
Epiphany, NYPL (1907)
Hamilton Fish Park, NYPL (1909)
High Bridge, NYPL (1908)
Hudson Park, NYPL (1906)
Hunt's Point, NYPL (1929)
Melrose, NYPL (1914)
Muhlenberg, NYPL (1906)
Port Richmond, NYPL (1905)
Riverside, NYPL (1905)
St. George, NYPL (1907)
Stapleton, NYPL (1904)
Tottenville, NYPL (1904)
Tremont, NYPL (1905)
Washington Heights, NYPL (1914)

MCKIM, MEAD & WHITE
Chatham Square, NYPL (1903)
Fordham, NYPL (1923)
Hamilton Grange, NYPL (1907)
Harlem, NYPL (1909)
Knightsbridge, NYPL (1905)
115h Street, NYPL (1908)
125th Street, NYPL (1904)
Rivington, NYPL (1905)
St. Gabriel's Park, NYPL (1908)
Schomburg, NYPL (1905)
Tompkins Square, NYPL (1904)
Woodstock, NYPL (1914)

COOK & WELCH
Fort Washington, NYPL (1914)
West 40th Street, NYPL (1913)

R.L. DAUS/DAUS & OTTO
Flatbush, BPL (1905)
Greenpoint, BPL (1906)
Saratoga, BPL (1908)
Walt Whitman, BPL (1908)

HEINS & LAFARGE
Poppenhusen, QBPL (1904)

HERTS & TALLANT
Aguilar, NYPL (1905)

JAMES BROWN LORD
Yorkville, NYPL (1902)

LORD & HEWLETT
Bedford, BPL (1905)
Brownsville, BPL (1908)
Fort Hamilton, BPL (1907)
South, BPL (1905)
Elmhurst, QBPL (1906)
Far Rockaway, QBPL (1904)
Flushing, QBPL (1906)

WILLIAM B. TUBBY/TUBBY BROS
Carroll Gardens, BPL (1905)
DeKalb, BPL (1905)
Leonard, BPL (1908)
Stone, BPL (1914)

TUTHILL & HIGGINS
Astoria, QBPL (1904)
Richmond Hill, QBPL (1905)

ROBERT F. SCHIRMER
Woodhaven, QBPL (1924)

EDWARD TILTON
Washington Irving, BPL (1923)

**RICHARD A. WALKER/
WALKER & MORRIS**
Arlington, BPL (1906)
Macon, BPL (1907)
Red Hook, BPL (1915)
Williamsburg, BPL (1905)

ORIGINAL BUILDERS

John T. Brady & Company

Brownsville, BPL, (Lord & Hewlett)
Fort Hamilton, BPL (Lord & Hewlett)
Hamilton Fish Park, NYPL (Carrere & Hastings)
High Bridge, NYPL (Carrere & Hastings)
Hudson Park, NYPL (Carrere & Hastings)
Red Hook, BPL (Walker)

Thomas J. Brady Company

Columbus, NYPL (Babb, Cook & Willard)
115th Street, NYPL (McKim, Mead & White)

Luke A. Burke & Sons

Eastern Parkway, BPL (Almirall)

P.J. Carlin & Company

Greenpoint, BPL (Daus)

Richard Carman

Far Rockaway, QBPL (Lord & Hewlett)

Church Construction Company

Pacific, BPL (Almirall)
Park Slope, BPL (Almirall)
South, BPL (Lord & Hewlett)

William L. Crow Construction Company

Fordham, NYPL (McKim, Mead & White)
Fort Washington, NYPL (Cook & Welch)
Mott Haven, NYPL (Babb, Cook & Willard)
Saratoga, BPL (Daus)
67th Street, NYPL (Babb, Cook & Willard)
Walt Whitman (BPL (Daus)

Richard Deeves & Company

Morrisania, NYPL (Babb, Cook & Willard)
Seward Park, NYPL (Babb, Cook & Welch)
West 40th Street, NYPL (Cook & Welch)
Woodstock, NYPL (McKim, Mead & White)

F.G. Fearon Company

Washington Irving, BPL (Tilton)

Fraser & Berau

Woodhaven, QBPL (Robert F. Schirmer)

General Building & Construction Co.

Aguilar, NYPL (Herts & Tallant)

Isaac Hopper & Son

96th Street, NYPL (Babb, Cook & Willard)
St. Agnew, NYPL (Babb, Cook, & Willard)
Yorkville, NYPL (James Brown Lord)

F.J. Kelley's Sons

DeKalb, BPL (Tubby)
Leonard, (BPL (Tubby)
Stone, BPL (Tubby)

Robert J. Mahoney

Bedford, BPL (Lord & Hewlett)

Norcross Brothers & Company

Washington Heights, NYPL (Carrere & Hastings)

Edwin Outwater

Melrose, NYPL (Carrere & Hastings)

E.E. Paul Company

Epiphany, NYPL (Carrere & Hastings)
58th Street, NYPL (Babb, Cook & Willard)
Hunt's Point, NYPL (Carrere & Hastings)
Muhlenberg, NYPL (Carrere & Hastings)
Port Richmond, NYPL (Carrere & Hastings)
Riverside, NYPL (Carrere & Hastings)
Stapleton, NYPL (Carrere & Hastings)
Tottenville, NYPL (Carrere & Hastings)

H.F. Quinn & Sons

Elmhurst, QBPL (Lord & Hewlett)

Michael Reid & Company

Chatham Square, NYPL (McKim, Mead & White)
Hamilton Grange, NYPL (McKim, Mead & White)
Harlem, NYPL (McKim, Mead & White)
Kingsbridge, NYPL (McKim, Mead & White)
125th Street, NYPL (McKim, Mead & White)
Rivington, NYPL (McKim, Mead & White)
St. Gabriel's Park, NYPL (McKim, Mead & White)
Schomburg, NYPL (McKim, Mead & White)
Tompkins Square, NYPL (McKim, Mead & White)

Remington Construction Company

Williamsburg, BPL (Walker & Morris)

Daniel Ryan

Macon, BPL (Walker & Morris)

John W. Schaefer, Jr. & Company

Bushwick, BPL (Almirall)
Tremont, NYPL (Carrere & Hastings)

L.W. Seaman Company

Arlington, BPL (Walker & Morris)

John Thatcher & Son

Carroll Gardens, BPL (Tubby)
Flatbush, BPL (Daus)

J.C. Vreeland Building Company

St. George, NYPL (Carrere & Hastings)
Webster, NYPL (Babb, Cook & Willard)

Thomas Williams

Flushing, QBPL (Lord & Hewlett)
Poppenhusen, QBPL (Heins & LaFarge)

Unknown

Astoria, QBPL (Tuthill & Higgins)
Richmond Hill, QBPL (Tuthill & Higgins)

1901 AGREEMENT BETWEEN THE NEW YORK PUBLIC LIBRARY AND THE CITY OF NEW YORK

The New York Public Library,
Astor, Lenox and Tilden Foundations.

AGREEMENT

ENTERED INTO WITH THE

CITY OF NEW YORK

RELATIVE TO THE GIFT OF

ANDREW CARNEGIE

FOR

BRANCH FREE CIRCULATING LIBRARY BUILDINGS

17 JULY, 1901

This Agreement, made and concluded this Seventeenth day of July, in the year of one thousand nine hundred and one, by and between THE CITY OF NEW YORK, by the BOARD OF ESTIMATE AND APPORTIONMENT of said City, party of the first part, and THE NEW YORK PUBLIC LIBRARY, ASTOR, LENOX AND TILDEN FOUNDATIONS, party of the second part, Witnesseth:

Whereas, Andrew Carnegie, of the City of New York, has heretofore offered to furnish the funds necessary for the erection of buildings for 65 free branch libraries for circulation in the City of New York, estimated in all to cost the sum of five million two hundred thousand dollars ($5,200,000), being an average cost of $80,000 each, provided the City of New York would furnish the necessary sites for such buildings and agree in satisfactory form to provide for the maintenance of said branches when completed, and

Whereas, by an Act of the Legislature of the State of New York, approved April 26th, 1901, entitled "An Act to authorize" and empower the City of New York to establish and maintain "a free public library system," being Chapter 580 of the Laws of 1901, the Board of Estimate and Apportionment of the City of New York is authorized in its discretion to acquire title by gift, condemnation or purchase to sites for free branch public libraries for circulation, with the approval of the person or corporation with whom the contract is made, for the erection of buildings thereon; and whereby such Board is further empowered upon the terms and conditions imposed in said act to authorize the use of any real estate belonging to the City of New York which is not required for other public purposes, for the maintenance and erection of said free public branches; and by which act the said Board of Estimate and Apportionment is further authorized in its discretion to make and enter into contracts with said Andrew Carnegie, or with any person or persons designated by him or with his personal representative, or with any corporation or corporations approved by him or them having lawful authority to construct and maintain free libraries, for the erection and equipment without cost to the City of New York of library buildings upon such sites so to be acquired, or upon sites now possessed or which may hereafter be possessed by any corporation with which such contract is made, or by the City of New York, and which Board of Estimate and Apportionment is further authorized to provide in such contracts for the maintenance of public library system in the City of New York, including therein the maintenance of any or all of the free public libraries now existing in said city which have heretofore been maintained in whole or in part by the public funds of said city, as well as for the maintenance of said branch libraries so to be erected as hereinbefore provided, and of traveling libraries, which amounts required for maintenance shall constitute a city charge to be provided for in the annual budget and tax levy of said City of New York, and which contracts may provide for the maintenance of the libraries to be constructed on such sites as rapidly as the same may be obtained and library buildings are erected thereon; and

Whereas, it is not at the present time deemed expedient by the parties hereto to avail of so much of said act of the Legislature as relates to the incorporation in this agreement of provisions for the support of free public libraries now existing in said City which have heretofore been maintained in whole or in part by the public funds of said City, but rather to leave that subject to be disposed of as the same may from time to time arise hereafter; and

Whereas, the said The New York Public Library, Astor, Lenox and Tilden Foundations has been approved by said Andrew Carnegie, as provided in said act, and duly designated by him as his agent for the purpose of this agreement, and has lawful authority to construct and maintain free libraries in the City of New York; and

Whereas, it is desired by the said party of the first part to avail of the offer of said Andrew Carnegie upon the terms provided in said act of the Legislature hereinabove referred to, and upon the terms and in the manner herein set forth.

Now, therefore, it is agreed between the said parties hereto as follows, viz:

First: The party of the first part shall proceed to acquire title by gift, purchase or by condemnation, as provided in said Act hereinbefore referred to, to such sites as shall be necessary in the Boroughs of Manhattan, the Bronx and Richmond, for the purpose of the erection and maintenance thereon of free branch public libraries, on the approval in each case of the said The New York Public Library, Astor, Lenox and Tilden Foundations, which sites so to be selected and approved shall not, unless by mutual consent, exceed in number forty-two in the said Boroughs of Manhattan, The Bronx and Richmond, the proportion of said Sixty-five Libraries allotted to said Boroughs; and the said Board of Estimate and Apportionment of the City of New York, by resolution adopted by the unanimous vote of said Board and approved by the unanimous vote of the Commissioners of the Sinking Fund of the City of New York, and on the approval in each case of The New York Public Library, Astor, Lenox and Tilden Foundations, may authorize the use of any real estate belonging to said City of New York, which is not required for other public purpose of such erection and maintenance; and further provided that any site now possessed or hereafter acquired by the said The New York Public Library, Astor, Lenox and Tilden Foundations, may, with the approval of the said Board of Estimate and Apportionment, be used as a site for the erection and maintenance of such branch public libraries as aforesaid.

Second: The New York Public library, Astor, Lenox and Tilden Foundations, shall upon the acquisition of title to any site so approved as aforesaid, or upon the passage of resolutions as aforesaid by the unanimous vote of the members of the Board of Estimate and Apportionment and of the said Commissioners of the Sinking Fund, authorizing the use of any real estate of the City of New York, not required for other public purposes, or upon the approval of the Board of Estimate and Apportionment of any site now possessed or which may hereafter be possessed or acquired by the party of the second part, proceed with the erection and equipment of library buildings thereon, without cost to the City of New York, and shall complete the same with funds so to be contributed by Andrew Carnegie as aforesaid; provided, however, that the said The New York Public Library, Astor, Lenox and Tilden Foundations, shall not be required to, nor shall it, without the consent of the said Board of Estimate and Apportionment, commence the erection and equipment of a larger number than ten library buildings upon sites furnished by the City of New York in the Boroughs of Manhattan, The Bronx and Richmond, in any single calendar year under the provisions hereof, and not to exceed forty-two branch library buildings in all in the Boroughs of Manhattan, The Bronx and Richmond. Such sites and each of them and the buildings thereon when complete shall be devoted to the maintenance of free branch public circulating libraries and reading-rooms, and the same and each of the same are hereby set apart for use as free branch public libraries for circulation; and the said party of the first part does hereby grant, demise and let unto the said The New York Public Library, Astor, Lenox and Tilden Foundations and its successors, on the erection of such buildings in each case, the land or real estate so acquired for sites, and the said land or real estate, the use of which shall have been authorized by the said Board of Estimate and Apportionment and the Commissioners of the Sinking Fund of the City of New York, which is not required for any other public purpose, with all improvements upon the same or any of the same, together with the appurtenances; TO HAVE AND TO HOLD the same in each case unto the said party of the second part and its successors so long as the said party of the second part and its successors shall continue to maintain upon the same respectively free branch public libraries and readingÑrooms, and so long as the said party of the second part and its successors shall keep, perform and observe the covenants and conditions herein contained on its part to be kept, performed and observed.

Third: The party of the second part agrees forthwith upon the acquisition of any site by the City of New York when approved as hereinbefore provided, or when the use of any real estate belonging to the City of New York which is not required for any other public purposes, shall have been duly granted as aforesaid, when approved by the party of the second part, or upon the approval of any site now possessed or to be hereafter possessed by the party of second part by the Board of Estimate and Apportionment of the City of New York as a site for a free public library for circulation within the meaning of the above mentioned act, to proceed to erect upon the same respectively branch libraries for circulation, and to equip the same, the expense thereof to be paid from funds to be furnished by Andrew Carnegie, and without cost to the City of New York; and the party of the second part further agrees to complete the same as soon as possible, and thereafter to conduct and carry on in the same respectively, with funds to be provided by the party of the first part as hereinafter provided, free public libraries for circulation with reading rooms, and to devote the same to the use of the public.

Fourth: The party of the first part further agrees adequately to provide for the maintenance of the free public branch libraries to be erected pursuant to this agreement, and of traveling libraries, in said city, and to that end to provide in each year in the annual budget and tax levy of said City a sum not less than ten per centrum of the amount expended by said Andrew Carnegie under the provisions of said Act, which sum shall be expended for the maintenance of the branch libraries to be hereafter constructed pursuant to this contract, which maintenance shall be provided for said libraries to be hereafter constructed as rapidly as the same are obtained; and in case a library building is under construction, maintenance may be provided therefor, to commence when constructed; and provided further that the obligation hereby assumed by the party of the first part to provide for such maintenance a sum not less than ten per centrum of the amount so expended by said Andrew Carnegie, shall not be taken to limit the right of said Board of Estimate and Apportionment to appropriate for such maintenance any larger sum if, in its discretion, additional appropriations should be required.

Fifth: The party of the second part further agrees that such amounts so to be appropriated in each year for the maintenance of a free public library system in the Boroughs of Manhattan, The Bronx and Richmond shall be applied solely to the maintenance of the several branch public libraries for circulation constructed therein pursuant to the terms of this agreement.

Sixth: IT IS FURTHER AGREED that the said several branch libraries which may be constructed pursuant to the provisions of said act, and each of them, shall be accessible at all reasonable hours and times, free of expense, to the persons resorting thereto, subject only to such reasonable control and regulation as the party of the second part, its successors or successor, from time to time may exercise and establish for general convenience; provided further that the lending, delivery and one or more reading rooms in each of said library buildings shall be open and accessible to the public upon every day of the week except Sunday, but including all legal holidays, from at least nine o'clock A.M. to at least nine o'clock P.M., under such rules and regulations as the said party of the second part shall prescribe from time to time, and on Sundays such parts of any of such libraries may be opened in such manner and during such hours as may be from time to time agreed upon between the said Board of Estimate and Apportionment and said The New York Public Library, Astor, Lenox and Tilden Foundations.

Seventh: The books contained in said several libraries which shall be purchased with funds provided by said Andrew Carnegie or by funds hereafter provided by the City of New York shall be and remain the property of the City of New York and shall be marked plainly as such, and the authorities of the City of New York shall have at all time access to every part of said library buildings and libraries and each of them, for general police visitation and supervision, and also for the purpose of the performance of the duties devolving upon them by the laws of the State of New York now or hereafter to be enacted, and the police powers exercised by the said City of New York shall extend in, through and over the said buildings and each of them. The party of the second part, however, shall appoint, direct, control and remove all persons employed within the said buildings respectively and in the care of the same. All fines to be exacted from any person or persons shall be retained by the party of the second part, applied to the business of circulation and duly accounted for in its accounts. All balances of annual appropriations by the party of the first part and not duly expended by the party of the second part for the maintenance of such libraries during the calendar years for which such appropriations shall have been made, shall be accounted for and paid by the said of the second part to the Comptroller of the City of New York to be deposited to the credit of the general fund for the reduction of taxation within sixty days after the expiration of each of such calendar years.

Eighth: The City shall annually, in addition to the provision for maintenance heretofore provided for, provide funds for the repair of the several buildings located upon sites owned by or furnished by the City. The City, in addition, shall at all times furnish a supply of water, and with the limitations already defined the party of the second part shall exercise direction and management over the affairs of the several library buildings, and the books, collections, and appurtenances.

Ninth: It is further agreed that this agreement may be wholly canceled or annulled, or form time to time altered or modified, as to any one or more of the library buildings hereafter to be constructed or owned or for which maintenance is provided under the provisions of this agreement, as may be agreed upon in writing between the parties hereto or their successors, anything herein to the contrary notwithstanding.

Tenth: That the said party of the second part shall on or before the first day of May in every year during the continuance of this agreement submit to the party of the first part, its successor or successors, a detailed report of the transactions of the party of the second part, to and including the 31st day of December of the year preceding.

In witness whereof, the party of the first part has caused this agreement to be executed by the Board of Estimate and Apportionment pursuant to resolution adopted at a meeting held on the Seventeenth day of July, 1901, and the party of the second part has caused this agreement to be executed by its President, and its official seal to be hereto affixed pursuant to resolutions of the Trustees of the New York Public Library, Astor, Lenox and Tilden Foundations, and adopted at a meeting held on the 29th day of May, 1901.

ROBT. A. VAN WYCK,
Mayor.

BIRD S. COLER,
Comptroller.

JOHN WHALEN,
Corporation Counsel.

RANDOLPH GUGGENHEIMER,
President of the Council.

THOS. L. FEITNER,
*President of the Department of
Taxes and Assessments.*

THE NEW YORK PUBLIC LIBRARY, ASTOR, LENOX
AND TILDEN FOUNDATIONS:

BY JOHN BIGELOW,
President.

[CORPORATE SEAL.]

Attest:
G. L. Rives,
Secretary.